THE SINGLE GUY COOKBOOK

PAGE STREET
PUBLISHING CO.

AVI SHEMTOV

FOUNDER OF THE CHUBBY CHICKPEA FOOD TRUCK

THE SINGLE GUY COOKBOOK

HOW TO COOK COMFORT FOOD FAVORITES FASTER, EASIER AND CHEAPER THAN GOING OUT

PAGE STREET
PUBLISHING CO.

Copyright © 2015 Avi Shemtov

First published in 2015 by
Page Street Publishing Co.
27 Congress Street, Suite 103
Salem, MA 01970
www.pagestreetpublishing.com

All rights reserved. No part of this book may be reproduced or used, in any form or by any means,
electronic or mechanical, without prior permission in writing from the publisher.

Distributed by Macmillan; sales in Canada by The Canadian Manda Group; distribution in Canada by
The Jaguar Book Group.

18   17   16   15   1   2   3   4   5

ISBN-13: 978-1-62414-115-7
ISBN-10: 1-62414-115-3

Library of Congress Control Number: 2014957749

Cover and book design by Page Street Publishing Co.
Photography by Ken Goodman

Printed and bound in China

Page Street is proud to be a member of 1% for the Planet. Members donate one percent of
their sales to one or more of the over 1,500 environmental and sustainability charities across
the globe who participate in this program.

This book is dedicated to all the chefs who make Boston's food truck scene such an incredible environment to work in, most specifically David Harnik, Rich Cambriello, Geo Lambert, Kevin McGuire, James DiSabatino, Irene, Andy & Mei Li, Adam Gendreau and Patrick Gilmartin. You all inspire me to be great and to make food that cool ass people want to eat.

INTRODUCTION

For as long as I can remember, food has been my passion. My dad is a chef, and when I was growing up, I thought that was so cool. The funny thing is, I never really watched him cook in any of his restaurants—I would just hang out with my sister in the basement or whatever backroom had a TV. Where I really enjoyed watching him was in our kitchen at home.

My dad believed he could cook anything. Both self-taught and professionally trained, in equal measures, he specialized in Turkish peasant food and Israeli street fare. These would later become my professional pursuits as well. But at home, he was a Chinese line cook, a short-order at a greasy spoon, even the *chef de cuisine* at a five-star French bistro. Those are all the guys I wanted to become.

By the time I was eight, I was already waking up the household with blueberry pancakes on Saturday morning, sometimes with the help of the smoke alarms. During middle school, I started pickling vegetables and making my own mustard. When I was in high school, I got a summer job washing dishes and prepping at a conference center. We'd play ball, wash dishes and make over-the-top staff meals.

My college buddies are often the beneficiaries of my love of kitchen work: Whether we are chowing down on ribs at a tailgate or eating a bizarre (but really, really good!) puff pastry omelet during a blizzard in D.C., I am serving up something that everyone else wants to know how to make. Now that we all have graduated to the real world and have started watching things like bank accounts and waistlines, my cooking advice has changed with the times. Our conversations have started to revolve around nutrition, grocery shopping and how to cook a four-star entree at home for the girl one of my friends has just met. And though I am not single myself anymore, I'm still the go-to for all my single buddies looking for an easy recipe.

For my gym-rat friends, the most important thing was coming up with food that tasted awesome but didn't have a ton of salt, fat, carbs, and the other stuff that restaurants use to make stuff taste, well, awesome. The cost conscious crew members? They were always curious to see what could be made for very little but would go over big. What everyone really wanted, though, was an array of meals that were easy to make, didn't take very long, tasted awesome, and didn't cost an arm and a leg.

Single guys like you have plenty of things to worry about—work, women, fantasy football—and the last thing you want is a collection of long, complicated recipes. In this book I've given you the same easy-to-make (and clean up), great-tasting recipes that I've passed along to my buddies. What I've always believed makes food taste great is creativity, fresh ingredients and a passion for flavor—and you will get all that out of here. Time to cut a few onions and grab a pan.

NO SHIRT, NO SHOES

CHAPTER ONE

FASTER AND CHEAPER THAN GOING OUT

Some of the best food I've ever eaten has come from the kitchens of great home cooks; I've always believed that a home-cooked meal can be every bit as good as a restaurant's. Lo mein made with fresh veggies and Chinese sausage (p. 13) is so good, you'll wince at the thought of takeout. Mac and cheese with steak and seafood (p. 40)? Kick-ass grub without having to make reservations. Try the tuna melt, too (p. 16)—it's as good as it gets. These recipes are meant to replace meals you'd have to open your closet and wallet to eat. Enjoy them from the comfort of your very own kitchen.

THE ONE GUY STIR-FRY

A stir-fry is the ultimate healthy, quick and fresh dinner, and this one makes a complete one-man meal. If carbs are a no-no, just get rid of the rice noodles and check out the tofu noodles in the produce section of your supermarket. If you go that route, however, add the noodles with the steak because they'll need a lot longer to dry out, or they'll taste like tofu!

MAKES 1 SERVING

1 cup (90 g) rice noodles

2 tbsp (30 ml) sesame oil

1 (5-oz [142-g]) shoulder steak, cut into strips

½ cup (90 g) chopped broccoli

½ cup (50 g) snow peas

1 carrot, peeled and chopped fine

½ white onion, cut into rings

1 tbsp (15 ml) low-sodium soy sauce

Bring a pot of water to a boil and drop in the rice noodles. Boil for 1 or 2 minutes and drain them well.

In a very large frying pan or a wok, if you have one, heat the sesame oil over high heat. Put in steak strips and cook, using a wooden spoon to keep the meat moving constantly, so it doesn't burn. When the steak is browned, about 2 minutes, add the broccoli, snow peas, carrots and onions. Cook, stirring, for 3 to 4 minutes, or until the veggies have softened.

Add the soy sauce and rice noodles. Mix everything up and continue cooking for about 2 minutes, or until the noodles are hot. Dump the stir-fry onto a plate and eat.

CHINESE SAUSAGE LO MEIN

Anyone who knows me knows better than to hand me the phone for a late-night Chinese food order if we've gotten pretty banged up. But I'm pretty sure my buddy Coco hands me the phone on purpose, knowing we'll end up with everything he likes, too! This lo mein recipe combines those tasty sparerib-style sausages, which became so popular a few summers ago, with the undeniable beauty of fresh lo mein. If you happen to have a bunch of veggies around, go nuts—I try to keep the ingredient lists short for those of us who don't keep weird stuff around unless we need it.

MAKES 1 LARGE SERVING

SAUCE

1½ tsp (7 ml) sesame oil
1 tbsp (15 ml) soy sauce
Pinch of sugar
Pinch of ground ginger (optional)

4 oz (115 g) lo mein egg noodles
1½ tsp (7 ml) sesame oil
½ red bell pepper, sliced thin
½ green bell pepper sliced thin
2 cloves garlic, minced
¼ cup (17 g) mushrooms, sliced (optional)
2 Chinese sausages links, chopped

Use a fork to mix together the sesame oil, soy sauce, sugar and ginger (if using) in a small bowl. Put this aside for a few minutes

Cook the noodles in a pot of boiling water according to the instructions on the package, and drain them well. Set aside.

Pour the sesame oil into a large frying pan over medium-high heat. After giving it a minute to get hot, throw the peppers, garlic and mushrooms (if using) into the oil and cook, stirring them often, for 2 minutes, or until they start to soften. Add the Chinese sausage and cook for 3 to 4 more minutes, stirring often.

Once the sausages are browned, add the noodles and sauce to the pan. Cook, stirring for about 1 minute, or until the noodles and sauce are warm. Pour everything into a large bowl and eat.

CHEESY SAUSAGE POTATOES

Here is a delicious way to combine greasy sausage with two other favorites—cheese and potatoes—and keep it simple and cheap at the same time. Almost all of the work is done by the oven; all you have to do is cut the potatoes, mix up the sauce, watch SportsCenter and then dig into all that melted cheese!

MAKES 1 SERVING

2 russet potatoes, peeled and sliced thin
1 small onion, peeled and sliced thin

SAUCE
3 tbsp (45 g) butter
2 cups (460 g) chopped sausage links
3 tbsp (23 g) all-purpose flour
1½ cups (355 ml) milk
1 tbsp (16 g) brown mustard
½ cup (56 g) shredded Colby Jack cheese

Preheat the oven to 375°F (191°C). Spray the inside of a baking pan with nonstick cooking spray. Cover the bottom of the pan with the potato slices and scatter the onion over the potatoes.

In a large saucepan, melt the butter over medium heat. Add the sausage and cook, stirring often so it doesn't burn, for about 3 minutes or until the sausage is lightly browned. Mix in the flour, and keep stirring until you have a smooth paste. Add the milk, stirring and until the sauce is smooth. Add the mustard and cook, stirring the whole time, for about 5 minutes or until the sauce starts to thicken. Add the cheese and stir for another minute, or until the sauce is smooth.

Pour the cheese sauce over the potatoes and onions and cover the pan with foil. Bake for 50-60 minutes, or until you can pierce the potatoes with a fork really easily. Transfer to a plate and eat.

SPICY PASTA & CHICKEN SALAD

Orzo is an awesome pasta to use for pasta salad because it cooks really fast and it's small, so you can mix almost anything into it. The other cool thing about orzo is that it's great hot or cold. This recipe is so good because it uses tangy banana peppers for a little bite, always-on-the-money rotisserie chicken from the grocery store and some fresh herbs for a great home-cooked touch! By the way, I like the dark meat, but you can take the meat from any part of the chicken you want.

MAKES 1 SERVING

4 cups (950 ml) water

1 cup (170 g) orzo

¼ cup (43 g) chopped banana peppers

¼ cup (40 g) diced vine-ripe tomatoes

1 tsp (5 ml) olive oil

¼ cup (10 g) chopped fresh flat-leaf parsley

¼ cup (45 g) chopped green olives

1 cup (125 g) chopped cooked chicken, such as rotisserie chicken

1 tbsp (8 g) paprika

Pinch of cayenne pepper

Pinch of salt

Pour the water into a medium-size pot and bring to a boil over high heat. Add the orzo and let it boil until tender, about 5 to 7 minutes, stirring it occasionally while it cooks to keep it from clumping. Drain the orzo well and return it to the empty pot or transfer it to a mixing bowl.

Add the remaining ingredients, mix the pasta salad really well and eat.

TUNA MIND MELT

Every time I make this sandwich, I think of chef Josh Smith, one of the most inspiring people I've ever met in the food business. As he served me a jaw-dropping dish he said, "If there's a way to do it, overdo it." This sandwich is made in that spirit. Sub in perfectly cooked fresh tuna for the canned version, melt some great cheese, get some fresh bread (instead of the stuff sitting on the shelf) and add all of the toppings you want. You don't have to complicate it if you don't want. You can just cook a tuna steak and mix it with mayo and some seasonings. Remember, though: Don't just do it, overdo it!

MAKES 1 LARGE SERVING

1 tsp (5 ml) olive oil

1 (8-oz [230-g]) tuna steak

1 bakery-fresh torpedo roll or another long sandwich roll

¼ cup (56 ml) real mayo or Miracle Whip

4 slices of sharp cheddar cheese (or your favorite)

2 tbsp (20 g) dry unseasoned bread crumbs

¼ cup (38 g) chopped white onion (optional)

1 tsp (5 g) salt

1 tsp (2 g) black pepper

2 slices tomato

2 romaine lettuce leaves, cut into shreds (optional)

¼ cup (43 g) chopped banana peppers (optional)

1 kosher dill pickle, quartered lengthwise (optional)

Preheat the oven to 350°F (177°C).

Heat the olive oil in a large frying pan over medium heat for about 45 seconds. Using electric? Give it 45 minutes—that's a joke. Give it 1 or 2 minutes; an electric burner takes longer to heat a pan. When the oil is hot, put the tuna in the pan and brown on one side for 1 minute or so. Flip it—this is the easiest step of the whole recipe—throw a cover on the pan, and let the tuna cook all the way through, 5–8 minutes, depending on how hot your stove runs and how thick the tuna is. The tuna should be cooked through and tender enough to flake apart with a fork. Remove from the heat and set aside.

With a serrated blade, cut the torpedo in half lengthwise, leaving a hinge. Don't cut all the way through dude; you want a sub, not sloppy joe of the sea. Open up the roll and spread each side with 1 tablespoon (14 ml) of the mayo. Place 2 slices of cheese on each side and put the roll into the oven—on a baking sheet, please! Bake, checking every minute or so, until the cheese is gooey.

In a large bowl, flake the tuna (mash it up) with a fork, and add the remaining 2 tablespoons (28 ml) of the mayo. Add the bread crumbs, and if you wish, the onion. Season with the salt and pepper. Using the same fork, mix the tuna until the ingredients are evenly distributed and all of the fish is broken up.

Place the sliced tomato on the bottom half of the roll, and scatter the lettuce on top, if you wish. Mound the tuna on top of the veggies, and if you like, scatter the banana peppers over the tuna. Top with the pickle and grub!

CHOCOLATE CHIP & BACON PANCAKES

Breakfast food is some of the cheapest and easiest comfort food around. Who doesn't love a sweet-and-savory, greasy breakfast after a rough night or to kick off a lazy day? Inspired by chocolate-covered bacon, which has been popping up all over the place, I created bacon and chocolate chip pancakes. Although pancake mixes are a shortcut, they don't eliminate enough steps for my money.

MAKES 1 SERVING (4 PANCAKES)

3 strips bacon
¾ cup (94 g) all-purpose flour
1½ tsp (6 g) baking powder
1 tbsp (15 g) unsalted butter, melted
1 tsp (4 g) brown sugar
½ cup (120 ml) milk
1 egg, lightly beaten with a fork
1 cup (180 g) chocolate chips

Cut the bacon strips in half crosswise and place them in a frying pan over medium-high heat. Cook for 2 to 3 minutes, or until brown on the bottom. Flip the bacon and cook until it has crisped up. With tongs, transfer the bacon to a paper towel to absorb the fat. Be careful! Bacon grease is very hot. When the bacon has cooled, crumble it up, put in a small bowl and set aside.

Combine the flour, baking powder, melted butter and brown sugar in a medium-size bowl. Stir in the milk and egg. Using a large spoon or whisk, or even better, an electric hand mixer, mix the ingredients until you have a smooth batter with no lumps. If you leave those lumps, your pancakes are not going to be good enough!

Spray a large frying pan with nonstick cooking spray or melt 1 tablespoon (14 g) of butter in the pan over medium-low heat and swirl it around to coat the pan. When the pan is hot, pour in about a quarter of the batter into the pan. Cook until little bubbles form on the surface of the pancake, about 45 seconds to 1 minute. Sprinkle a quarter of the bacon and a quarter of the chocolate chips over the pancake. After the pancake has begun to look firmer around the edges, about 30 seconds more, flip the pancake. Use a spatula—don't be a hero. Cook the second side for 1 to 2 minutes, or until done. Repeat these steps to make the remaining 3 pancakes.

HARD CIDER PORK CHOP

Pork Chops are great to cook for yourself and for friends because they're cheap and really easy to prepare. Baking an apple is also easy to do and adds sweetness, along with the hard cider, to the tender, juicy pork. Plus, the mushy baked apple makes for a great contrast with a fork full of the seared chop. This is a simple recipe for a very tasty dinner.

MAKES 1 SERVING

1 whole red apple, washed
1 tsp (5 ml) olive oil
1 bone-in pork chop
Pinch of salt
Pinch of black pepper
1 cup (240 ml) hard cider
1 tbsp (14 g) unsalted butter
1 tbsp (13 g) brown sugar

Preheat the oven to 400°F (204°C).

Put the apple in a baking pan or baking dish and bake until the insides are so mushy that you can see the apple imploding on itself, about 30 minutes. The apple should not offer any resistance at all when pressed with a pair of tongs. It's ready to rock.

While the apple bakes, heat the olive oil in a medium-size frying pan over medium-high heat. Season the pork chop with salt and pepper and brown it in the pan, 2 to 3 minutes per side. Add half of the hard cider, reduce the heat to medium-low, and cover the pan. Simmer the pork chop in the cider until the pork looks white all the way through, kind of like chicken, about 12–15 minutes. If you're feeling pro and have an instant-read thermometer around, 155°F (68°C) will work nicely. Take the chop out of the pan, leaving the grease and juice in the pan. Set the pan and chop aside.

When the apple is ready, use tongs or a fork to remove the skin. Scrape all of the pulp (but not the seeds) into the pan your chop was cooked in. Add the butter, brown sugar and the remaining cider to the pan and turn the heat to high. Cook, stirring with a wooden spoon so the mixture doesn't burn, until the apple pulp has browned a little and the cider has reduced to a sticky, sugary syrup, This will take only 1 or 2 minutes. Remove from the heat and scrape onto a dinner plate. Put your chop on top and bang, dinner is served!

CHEESY SAUSAGE FRENCH TOAST

The gourmet grilled cheese craze and the stuffed French toast craze are ready for an arranged marriage. There are only a few steps and the ingredients are cheap, so making extra for a friend isn't a problem. If you're in the mood for a hearty and savory breakfast with a little sweetness to it, this will definitely do the trick. The crispy outside, fluffy inside, greasy sausage, gooey cheese and sweet apple will start your day off right. You'll need to cut the sausages in half lengthwise while they're raw, which is a pain, but they'll cook much faster.

MAKES 2 STUFFED FRENCH TOASTS

½ cup (120 g) unsalted butter

1 apple, peeled and sliced

4 breakfast sausage links, halved lengthwise

2 eggs

1 tbsp (15 ml) milk

1 tsp (4 g) grated Parmesan cheese

4 thick slices challah bread

4 slices cheddar cheese

Preheat the oven to 375°F (191°C).

In a large frying pan over medium heat, melt 1 tablespoon (15 g) of the butter and add the apple. Cook, stirring the apple slices every few minutes to keep them from burning or sticking, for about 5 minutes, or until softened. Add the sausage to the pan and cook for 4 to 5 minutes, until cooked all the way through. Remove from the heat.

While the apples and sausages are cooking, crack your eggs into a large shallow bowl or a baking pan and add the milk and Parmesan. Use a fork to mix it all up, making sure the eggs are completely broken up.

On a baking sheet, arrange the bread slices side by side. Place a slice of cheese on each slice of bread. Divide the sausage halves between 2 of the bread slices. Arrange the apple slices over the sausage.

Clean out the frying pan and melt another 1 tablespoon (15 g) of the butter over medium heat. Use the slices of bread topped with only cheese to cover the bread with the sausage and apples, forming 2 sandwiches. Pick up a sandwich and dunk each side carefully into the egg mix. Place the sandwich in the hot butter and let it brown for 1 minute. Carefully flip the sandwich, using a spatula, and let the other side brown. Take out the sandwich and put it back on the baking sheet. Melt another 1 tablespoon (15 g) of butter in the pan and brown the second sandwich.

Put the baking sheet with the 2 sandwiches into the oven for 15 minutes. The bread will be crispy and the cheese will ooze. You're ready to eat.

STUPID-EASY POT ROAST

Some nights you just want beef, and lots of it. This pot roast has great flavor and is always tender. Plus it doesn't really need any attention (wish that was true about everything in your life, don't you?). Just come home, brown the sides and put it in the oven. By the time you're caught up on *Game of Thrones*, you'll have a tender block of meat to tear apart.

MAKES 2 SERVINGS

2 tbsp (30 ml) olive oil

8 oz (230 g) beef shoulder roast

1 cup (140 g) diced carrots

1 yellow onion, quartered

2 potatoes, quartered

1 tsp (5 g) salt

½ tsp cracked black pepper

1 tsp (2 g) ground cumin

1 tsp (2 g) ground coriander

Preheat oven to 375°F (191°C).

Heat the oil in a cast-iron skillet over high heat and quickly brown all sides of your meat, about 2 minutes per side. Remove from the heat.

Add the carrots, onion, potatoes and the seasonings. Cover the skillet with heavy-duty foil, sealing it completely, and place it in the oven. Cook for about 1 to 1½ hours, depending on how rare you like the meat.

The best part of this pot roast is how versatile it is. You can shred it and eat it on its own, have it on a roll with BBQ sauce and cole slaw or cut it into tender pieces and eat it over rice and its own juices.

MARY HAD A LITTLE STEW

Making stew is a great solution when you don't mind waiting but have a few things to get done before you eat. This recipe will take very little time to throw together; then the stove top will get the rest done for you. The stew is meaty and filling, too, and doesn't use very much of that pricey lamb to get the flavor lamb lovers crave. Oh, I almost forgot—you're only gonna have to wash one pan.

MAKES 2 LARGE SERVINGS

1 tbsp (15 ml) olive oil

1 white onion, diced

1 carrot, diced but not peeled

4 vine-ripe tomatoes, diced

1 potato, diced but not peeled

1 lb (455 g) lamb stew meat, cut into bite-size pieces

1 cup (240 ml) water

¼ cup (10 g) chopped fresh flat-leaf parsley

1 tsp (5 g) salt

1 tsp (2 g) black pepper

1 tsp (3 g) granulated garlic

1 tsp (2 g) cumin

Heat the olive oil in a medium-size saucepan over medium-high heat. Add the onion and carrot and cook, stirring occasionally, until the onions are translucent, about 4–5 minutes. Add the tomatoes, potato and lamb. Turn the heat down to medium and add the water, parsley, salt, pepper, garlic and cumin. Mix it up a little to blend the ingredients well.

Cover the stew and cook, checking on it every 5 minutes or so and adding water as needed to keep it from burning (but remember, you want it to be thick). The stew should be done in about 45 minutes, or when the lamb is tender enough to cut with a fork. You're ready to grub.

PLT—PROSCIUTTO, IT'S THE NEW BACON

I love a BLT because it's crunchy and creamy (the mayo), and has a meaty flavor. And I love prosciutto because it's super-thin and has just the right amount of fat. This recipe is so simple, but it's such a cool twist on an awesome classic that I really want you guys to have it in your arsenal. This sandwich is perfect when you're kicking around the house on Saturday morning after a rough night. Although it's greasy, it's not heavy, so you can still hit the gym.

MAKES 1 SERVING

1 tbsp (15 ml) olive oil
4 razor-thin slices of prosciutto
1 bakery-fresh baked roll
1 tbsp (14 ml) mayo
2 romaine lettuce leaves
½ vine-ripe tomato
2 slices cheddar cheese

Preheat the oven to 350°F (177°C).

Heat the olive oil and prosciutto in a medium-size frying pan over high heat. Cook for about 3 minutes, turning once, until the meat begins to crisp like bacon. Drain the prosciutto on paper towels.

Cut the roll in half along the equator. Spread the mayo on both sides of the open roll and put the lettuce on the bottom half. Cover with the prosciutto. Cut the tomato half into thin slices—although this won't make or break the sandwich—and layer the tomato over the meat. Add the cheddar last.

Close the sandwich and bake for about 7 minutes, or until the cheese has softened but is not completely melted. It's ready to eat.

SLOW-COOKER PULLED CHICKEN QUESADILLA

A slow cooker makes a crazy amount of fun possible and, more important, stupidly easy recipes. Sometimes I like to use the slow cooker to make an entire meal—like a stew—and sometimes I like to use it to make really tender meat for a dish I'm going to prepare later, such as this quesadilla. Pulled chicken is so simple to make, and it's the perfect protein for a quick-and-easy quesadilla. It's a great idea to get the chicken going in your slow cooker in the morning so you can make the quesadilla when you get home from work.

MAKES 1 SERVING

½ red onion

1 small green chile

2 medium-size chicken thighs (about 5 oz [140 g] each)

Pinch of salt

Pinch of black pepper

Pinch of granulated garlic

Pinch of ground cumin

1 cup (254 g) canned black beans, with their liquid

½ cup (120 ml) water

1 (12-in [30-cm]) flour tortilla

½ cup (56 g) shredded Monterey Jack cheese

½ vine-ripe tomato

Cut the red onion and green chile into small chunks, about ½-inch (13-mm) thick. Put the onion, chile, chicken thighs, salt, black pepper, garlic and cumin into your slow cooker. Add the black beans with their liquid from the can and the water. Set your slow cooker to medium and cook for 6 to 8 hours. If you don't have a slow cooker, you can preheat your oven to 225°F (107°C) and cook the same mixture in an ovenproof pot covered well with foil for 6 to 8 hours.

Once your chicken is ready, preheat the oven to 375°F (191°C). Put the tortilla on a baking sheet. Using a fork, remove the skin from the chicken thighs and pull the chicken off the bone. Put the pulled chicken, beans, onions and peppers on one half of the tortilla. Add the cheese, spreading it evenly across the chicken and veggies. Last, dice the tomato and put that on top of the cheese. Fold the tortilla so that it is a half-moon, fully stuffed, and bake for 15 to 20 minutes. Once the cheese is completely melted, you're ready to eat.

SHRIMP ENCHILADA

This recipe is a quick-and-easy way to cook shrimp, and a hands-off way to make a Mexican meal. If you want some good Mexican food without the hassle of making—or eating—tacos, this recipe is for you. And you can eat it with a fork!

MAKES 1 SERVING (2 MEAN ENCHILADAS)

¼ cup (60 g) unsalted butter

2 cloves garlic, minced

8 shrimp, peeled, deveined and chopped fine

½ cup (56 g) shredded Monterey Jack cheese

SAUCE

1 green chile, diced

½ white onion, diced small

1 vine-ripe tomato, diced

1 tsp (5 g) salt

½ tsp (1 g) black pepper

¼ cup (60 ml) Mexican lager beer, such as Corona Extra or Dos Equis

2 (6-in [15-cm]) corn tortillas

1 avocado

¼ cup (12 g) chopped scallion

Preheat the oven to 375°F (191°C).

First up, cook the shrimp. In a cast-iron or another type of frying pan, preferably an ovenproof one, melt the butter on medium-high heat. Add the garlic and the shrimp and use a wooden spoon to move them around so they don't burn. Add the shredded cheese and cook, stirring, for 2 to 3 minutes, or until the cheese has melted enough to hold the shrimp together. Transfer the mix to a bowl.

Leaving the pan on medium-high heat, add the chile, onion, tomato, salt, pepper and beer. Mix it all up and move it around every few minutes as it cooks down. Once the tomatoes are saucy, in about 12 to 15 minutes, remove from the heat. You're ready to put together your enchiladas.

Lay both corn tortillas flat on a plate. Cut the avocado lengthwise into eighths and divide evenly between the 2 tortillas. Pile the shrimp mix on top of the avocado and wrap the tortillas closed, with the seam on the bottom (where the ends meet, bro!). Place the enchiladas in the frying pan. Or, if your frying pan isn't ovenproof, transfer the enchiladas to a baking pan.

Pour the sauce over the enchiladas and bake for 10 to 12 minutes, or until the tortillas start to get crispy and the cheese is bubbly. Then you're ready to eat up.

OPEN-FACE SHRIMP PO' BOY

My last few days as a single man were spent at Mardi Gras with my buddies, celebrating my bachelorhood. Sure the bead tossing and booze in the streets were great, but some of the best moments of the trip were 3:00 a.m. po' boy sandwiches at hole-in-the-wall sammy shops. What a brilliant idea—fried fresh seafood on fresh bread with crispy veggies and mayo. How can you go wrong? This recipe features really easy lightly-fried shrimp, some liquid heat and fresh veggies.

MAKES 1 SERVING

2 cups (475 ml) canola oil

1 cup (125 g) all-purpose flour

1 cup (170 g) cornmeal

Pinch of salt

Pinch of cracked black pepper

2 cups shrimp, peeled, deveined

1 cup (85 g) coleslaw mix (veggies only!)

2 tsp (10 ml) hot sauce, such as Frank's RedHot

1 dill pickle, diced small

1 tsp (7 ml) honey

2 tbsp (28 ml) mayo

1 bakery-fresh French roll

1 tsp (2 g) Cajun seasoning

Heat the oil in a large frying pan over medium-high heat. While the oil is heating, in a medium-size bowl, mix together the flour, cornmeal, salt and black pepper. Put the shrimp in the bowl and toss them around so they're covered with the dry ingredients. After about 3 minutes, test the oil to see if it is hot enough: Put a pinch of flour into the oil. If it starts fizzing right away, add the shrimp. Fry for 4 minutes, turning them halfway through. To test for doneness, cut one open. It should be opaque, or a flat white, rather than shiny and clear. Transfer the shrimp to paper towels to dry.

Put your slaw mix in a medium-size bowl (you could empty and wash your flour bowl—efficiency!). Add the hot sauce, diced pickle, honey, and 1 tablespoon (14 ml) of the mayo. Mix the slaw thoroughly.

Cut the roll open, leaving it hinged. Open the roll on a plate so that it lays almost flat. Mix the remaining tablespoon (14 ml) of mayo and the Cajun seasoning together in a small bowl, and spread across both sides of the roll. Next heap the slaw over the bread. Finally, put the shrimp on top. This is probably more of a fork and knife meal than a sandwich. So snap a pic and get to work!

WASTED CHICKEN

If you like bourbon, this recipe will make your mouth water! It is one of the easiest recipes to follow, and the chicken will have the flavor of your favorite bourbon (Scotch or Cognac would work also) and a sweet, sticky sauce from the brown sugar. Make this when you come home from the gym. Set it all up in the pan and let it cook while you take a quick shower—it's that easy! This stuff is great on its own or over white or brown rice.

MAKES 1 SERVING

1 red bell pepper
½ white onion
1 tbsp (15 ml) olive oil
½ cup (30 g) baby bell mushrooms
1 tbsp (15 ml) bourbon
2 tsp (8 g) dark brown sugar
1 chicken breast (6–8 oz [170–230 g]), cut into ½-in-(13-mm-) thick strips

Cut the pepper and onion into thin strips. Heat the olive oil in a medium-size frying pan over medium heat. Add pepper, onion and mushrooms and use a wooden spoon to keep them moving so they don't burn. As the veggies begin to soften, in about 3 minutes or so, add the bourbon and brown sugar, mixing them in so that the sugar is not lumpy.

Add the chicken to the pan, reduce the heat to low, and cover the pan. Cook the chicken for about 10 minutes, or until cooked through. It's ready to eat.

SALMON TOSTADOS WITH BLACK BEAN SLAW

Tostados are a fun and easy way to eat any delicious mix of food. By frying the tortillas, you'll get a crunchy base for your meal, which is perfect for the fresh salmon and creamy black beans. Keep in mind that tostados will work with all sorts of toppings, so if salmon isn't on sale, you can fry up some chicken or beef and toss it on these crispy "crackers."

MAKES 1 SERVING (2 TOSTADOS)

SLAW

1 cup (85 g) coleslaw mix (veggies only!)

2 tbsp (5 g) chopped fresh cilantro

½ cup (128 g) canned black beans, rinsed and drained

Pinch of finely chopped Carolina Reaper chile, without seeds

1 tbsp (14 ml) mayo

Salt and black pepper to taste

Pinch of sugar

4-oz (115-g) salmon fillet

1 tbsp (15 ml) olive oil

2 (6-in [15-cm]) corn tortillas

½ avocado, diced

2 tablespoons (20 g) chopped tomato

2 tbsp (15 g) shredded Monterey Jack cheese

In a medium-size bowl, mix the coleslaw mix, cilantro, black beans, chile and mayo. Season with salt and pepper and add the sugar.

Fry the salmon fillet in a large nonstick pan (not my usual cast-iron, I know) for about 2 minutes on each side. Gently break apart into bite-size pieces and continue to panfry them, breaking them apart with a wooden spoon, until cooked through. Breaking apart the fish will give a great texture to the tostados and cook the fish completely. Set aside the fish and clean out the pan.

Return the pan to medium-high heat and heat the olive oil. Toss in the corn tortillas and crisp them up, about 1–2 minutes per side.

Transfer the tortillas to a plate, and top each one with half the slaw, and half the salmon. Top with avocado, tomato and cheese. Grub up!

SURF & TURF MAC & CHEESE

Mac and cheese is so much fun because it can be simple or complicated, and it can take on so many different flavors. You can even make some extra and fry the leftovers for a great snack or game-time grub. A quick-and-easy way to kick up a simple mac and cheese and make it a filling and tasty-as-hell comfort food is by adding great steak and simply seasoned shrimp.

MAKES 1 SERVING

1 cup (116 g) elbow macaroni

2 tsp (10 ml) olive oil

4 oz (115 g) sirloin tip

Salt and black pepper

1 cup (210 g) shrimp, deveined and peeled

½ cup (120 g) unsalted butter

2 tsp (5 g) all-purpose flour

1 cup (240 ml) cream (or milk in a pinch)

½ cup (60 g) cubed white cheddar cheese

Pinch of granulated garlic

Pinch of red pepper flakes (optional)

Fill a medium-size pot with water, and bring to a boil over high heat. Cook the macaroni according to the package directions until it is tender and ready to eat. Give it one stir after about 1 minute, to keep the macaroni from sticking. Drain and transfer to a large bowl or return to the pot.

Heat 1 teaspoon (5 ml) of the olive oil in a small frying pan over medium heat. After about 1 minute, season the sirloin tip with a pinch of salt and a pinch of black pepper and place it into the pan. Brown the meat well on each side, which will take about 1½ minutes. Remove the meat from the pan and set aside.

Season the shrimp with 1 teaspoon (5 g) of salt and 1 teaspoon (2 g) of pepper. Heat the remaining 1 teaspoon (5 ml) of olive oil in the pan over medium heat and add the shrimp. Cook the shrimp, covered, for about 2 minutes per side, or until pink all over and cooked through. Remove the shrimp from the pan and cut into small pieces. Do the same with the steak.

Melt the butter in a small saucepan over medium heat. Add the flour, 1 teaspoon (3 g) at a time, stirring constantly to make a paste. Drizzle in the cream, stirring away. You should have a creamy sauce. Add the cubed cheese and garlic and pepper flakes (if using) and season with salt and pepper. Cook, stirring, until the cheese has melted to form a thick cheese sauce.

Stir the cheese sauce and proteins into the macaroni, pile it on a plate and eat.

VEAL CUTLETS WITH ARTICHOKE HEARTS

Veal can be a little bit pricey, so look for really thin pieces. They'll cook quicker and easier, and they'll go a long way on short money! Remember, you're spending a lot less for a great meal at home than you would in a restaurant. Veal isn't really any more difficult to cook than steak, and the taste is much richer. The artichoke hearts pack a ton of flavor, too, don't require any work on your part and will kick your egg noodles up several notches.

MAKES 1 SERVING

1 cup (90 g) egg noodles
¼ cup (31 g) all-purpose flour
2 thin veal cutlets (scaloppine)
1 tbsp (15 ml) olive oil
2 tbsp (30 g) unsalted butter
1 tbsp (11 g) grated Parmesan cheese
½ cup (100 g) marinated artichoke hearts
Salt and black pepper to taste
¼ cup (10 g) chopped fresh flat-leaf parsley (optional)

Get a pot of water boiling and cook your noodles according to the instructions on the package. When they're done, drain them well and put them aside.

Put the flour in a shallow dish, and coat the veal cutlets in the flour to dry them out. Make sure every inch of meat is lightly floured. Heat the olive oil in a large frying pan over medium-high heat, add the veal and brown it for 2 minutes on each side. Remove the veal from the pan and drain on paper towels so any grease will drip off. Leave the pan on the heat!

Melt the butter in the pan and stir in the Parmesan. Add the artichoke hearts and season with salt and pepper. Cook, stirring with a wooden spoon, for 2 to 3 minutes to warm the artichokes and get the butter and cheese creamy. Add the egg noodles, stir until warm and remove from the heat.

Pour the pasta onto a plate, scraping out as much sauce as you can. Put the veal on top, garnish with some parsley (if using) and eat up.

WAFFLE-BATTERED CHICKEN TENDERS

Chicken and waffles is made with bone-in chicken and is eaten with hot sauce, real maple syrup and thick butter. I love it! This dish is more "chicken tender" than it is "chicken and waffles," but it's much easier and has got the same flavor, if you've got the ambition. Melt a little butter and stir it into some tangy BBQ sauce, and you might be able to capture the magic!

MAKES 4-6 TENDERS

½ cup (62 g) all-purpose flour

1 egg

¾ cup (180 ml) milk

2 tsp (7 g) baking powder

½ tsp vanilla extract

1 tsp (4 g) sugar

2 cups (475 ml) canola oil

8 oz (230 g) chicken tenders

1 tbsp (15 g) butter (optional)

2 tbsp (30 ml) BBQ sauce (optional)

Honey mustard sauce (optional)

In a medium-size bowl, mix the flour, egg, milk, baking powder, vanilla and sugar with a fork and continue mixing the batter until there are no lumps in it.

Heat the oil in a large frying pan over medium-high heat. After 4 to 5 minutes, test the oil by putting a few drops of batter in to see if it fries.

Put all of the tenders into the batter and coat them completely. Drop them into the oil and fry for 2 to 3 minutes per side, or until golden brown and cooked through. Your chicken is ready! Melt the butter and mix it with the BBQ sauce for an awesome dip, or stick with some honey mustard.

SIMPLE SPINACH PESTO AND CAMPANELLE PASTA

Spinach and grated Parmesan give pesto a great fresh and cheesy flavor and make a really filling sauce. Plus it's so quick and easy to make. The campanelle is a hearty pasta, and the pesto sticks to it well. You can kick it up to the next level by paying a visit to the olive bar at your grocery store. Grab 2 or 3 kalamata olives, a few pieces of roasted garlic, red pepper or artichokes and some interesting cheese and chop it all up. Add to the finished pasta for a real Mediterranean touch.

MAKES 1 LARGE SERVING

1 cup (116 g) campanelle pasta

3 cups (90 g) fresh spinach

⅓ cup (80 ml) olive oil

⅓ cup (40 g) dry unseasoned bread crumbs

1 tsp (5 g) salt

½ tsp black pepper

1 tsp (3 g) granulated garlic

½ cup (90 g) grated Parmesan cheese

¼ cup (60 ml) water, or as needed

1 tsp (5 g) butter, melted

Fill a medium-size pot with water and bring to a boil over high heat. Cook the campanelle according to the package directions, about 10 to 12 minutes, until it is tender and ready to eat. Drain and transfer to a large bowl or return to the pot.

Meanwhile, in a blender or food processor combine the spinach, olive oil, bread crumbs, salt, pepper, garlic and ¼ cup (45 g) of the Parmesan. Add water as needed to turn the paste into a sauce and keep the processor from jamming, 1 teaspoon (5 ml) at a time! Once the pesto has a smooth and saucelike consistency, you're all set.

Stir the butter into the pasta and add the pesto sauce, mixing it all together well. Put it in an individual bowl and top with the remaining ¼ cup (45 g) of Parmesan cheese.

NO MESS, NO STRESS

CHAPTER TWO

CLEAN UP-FREE MAN FOOD

What's the worst part of cooking a homemade meal? Having to clean up the kitchen when you're done, obviously. This chapter is dedicated to the situations where we need a delicious meal but don't want to spend an hour afterwards cleaning up after ourselves. Hearty Chili Seafood Chowder (p. 53) will take one pot and get eaten in one bowl. After your supper of Mind-Blowing Meatballs with Ziti (p. 49) your cleanup will be down to almost nothing. Some of these meals can even be eaten from the pan they're cooked in, like the Burger Bomb Bread Pudding (p. 68), for no dish washing. For the others, invest in some paper plates, and you'll be all set.

LAZY LASAGNA FOR 1

The first time I ever made fried lasagna balls, I didn't break the noodles up small enough and I ended up with a little mess. Thing is, that mess tasted really good, and it made me realize that lasagna could be made really easily. More importantly, it can be made in a small batch just right for one.

MAKES 1 SERVING

3 lasagna noodles
¼ cup (60 g) unsalted butter
4 oz (115 g) ground beef
1 cup (30 g) fresh spinach
1 tbsp (8 g) all-purpose flour
½ cup (120 ml) milk
¼ cup (28 g) shredded mozzarella
1 tbsp (14 g) ricotta cheese
½ cup (120 ml) traditional tomato sauce

Fill a medium-size pot with water and bring to a boil over high heat. Crack each lasagna noodle into 4 pieces and cook the noodles according to the package directions until tender and ready to eat. Drain and put them in a bowl.

In the pot you just used, melt the butter over medium heat and put the ground beef in. Cook, using a wooden spoon to break the meat apart and stirring until it starts to brown, about 4-5 minutes. Add the spinach and cook until the leaves wilt (get soggy), about 2–3 minutes. Add the flour and cook, stirring, until the whole mix gets kind of pasty, in about 1 minute. Add the milk gradually and cook, stirring some more, for about 1 more minute, or the mix becomes saucy. Add the mozzarella and ricotta and stir until the cheese melts into the mixture. Add the tomato sauce and cook, stirring for 30 seconds, just to warm it up.

Pour the meat, cheese and spinach mix over the noodles and stir it all up. Now you have a bowl of lasagna.

MIND-BLOWING MEATBALLS WITH ZITI

Some sauces need all day—no question—but sometimes great food can be made really quickly and without much equipment. This recipe leaves the skins on the tomatoes, cooks your sauce, meatballs and even your pasta in one pot, and in doing so lets the pasta really soak up the great flavors of the meat and tomato sauce. My favorite part is the texture you get cooking your meat and pasta in the sauce!

MAKES 1 HEAPING SERVING

4 vine-ripe tomatoes

2 tsp (10 ml) olive oil

1 tsp (1 g) dried basil

2 tsp (4 g) cracked pepper

1 tsp (4 g) sugar

2 tsp (10 g) salt

1 clove garlic, crushed with a fork and minced

¼ cup (30 g) dry unseasoned bread crumbs

1 tbsp (15 g) butter

¼ (60 ml) cup cream (or milk in a pinch)

4 oz (115 g) hot or sweet Italian sausage

4 oz (115 g) ground beef

1 cup (116 g) ziti

½ cup (120 ml) water

Cut the tomatoes into medium-size chunks. Heat the oil in a large frying pan over medium-high heat and add the tomatoes, basil, 1 teaspoon (2 g) of the cracked pepper, the sugar, 1 teaspoon (5 g) of the salt and the garlic. Give everything a stir with a wooden spoon. Once the liquid from the tomatoes begins to simmer, lower the heat to medium-low and cover the pan. Continue simmering the sauce (it should be bubbling gently) while you shape your meatballs, giving the sauce a stir every 3 to 4 minutes to make sure it isn't burning at the bottom. If you have to turn the heat down or add a little bit of water, feel free.

In a small bowl, mix the bread crumbs with the remaining 1 teaspoon (5 g) of the salt and 1 teaspoon (2 g) of the pepper, the butter and cream. The result should be kind of pasty. Now add the meats and mix until uniform. Your hands work the best for this; just wash them first! Divide the mix into 4 good-size meatballs and place them in the simmering sauce.

Add the ziti, making sure it is completely covered by the sauce, and stir in the water. Cover the pan and simmer the sauce for about 12 minutes, or until the pasta is al dente and the meatballs are tender and cooked through. Don't want to use a plate? Eating this over the counter out of the pan is cool, too. No judgments here!

KIELBASA CARBONARA

Carbonara is the classic comfort food—a greasy and creamy pasta dish with almost no ingredients and no fuss. In order to make it my own, I reached back to my childhood and combined it with the comfort food we ate in my house: Kielbasa. My dad would mix in paprika and throw it in a frying pan and use the beautiful grease it created to coat some pasta for a quick comfort dish. Kielbasa and spaghetti meet here, and the results are a greasy hug, in the best way.

MAKES 1 SERVING

1 cup (115 g) spaghetti
1 tsp (5 ml) olive oil
1 cup (33 g) (⅛-inch-[3-mm-] thick) sliced kielbasa
1 tsp (2 g) smoked paprika
2 eggs
¼ cup (45 g) grated Parmesan cheese
Pinch of salt
1 tsp (2 g) cracked black pepper

Fill a medium-size pot with water and bring to a boil over high heat. Cook the spaghetti according to the package directions until it is tender and ready to eat. Drain the pasta (don't run cold water over it) and return the hot pasta to the pot. Having your pasta hot is key if you want your eggs to cook and the sauce to get creamy.

While the spaghetti is cooking, heat the olive oil in a medium-size frying pan over medium-high heat. Add the kielbasa and paprika to the hot oil and cook, stirring the meat with a wooden spoon every 30 seconds to move it around. Once the kielbasa has browned and the pan is coated in kielbasa-and-paprika-flavored-grease, the kielbasa is done, about 3-4 minutes. Remove from the heat.

Crack the eggs into a small bowl, beat them lightly and whisk in the Parmesan cheese. Make sure your egg mixture has a smooth consistency.

Put the pot with the pasta over low heat and quickly add the kielbasa and grease, along with the salt and pepper. Use your stronger hand to stir the pasta rapidly while you pour the egg mix into the pot very slowly with your other hand. After about 45 seconds of stirring as hard as you can (so you don't get scrambled eggs), you should have a creamy and smoky sauce. Eat!

SPICY JALAPEÑO BREAD WITH SUNNY-SIDE UP EGGS

Sunny-side up eggs go great with a lot of things, with the yolk making a natural sauce or dip. This salty and spicy bread is very easy to make and the runny yolk gives it a biscuit-and-gravy-like quality.

MAKES 1 SERVING

2–3 eggs
¼ cup (60 ml) milk
¼ cup (33 g) biscuit mix, such as Bisquick
¼ cup (43 g) finely chopped jalapeño peppers
1 cup (120 g) shredded cheddar cheese

Preheat the oven to 375°F (191°C).

In a large bowl, use a fork to beat in 1 of the eggs, the milk and biscuit mix until smooth. Add the peppers and ¾ cup (90 g) of the cheese and stir them into the batter until well blended.

Transfer the batter to a small ovenproof dish or pan. You know what I'd use—my trusty cast-iron skillet. Bake for 25 to 30 minutes, or until the bread is light brown on top and a knife inserted in the middle comes out dry.

When the bread is done, pull it out and dig out a hole in the middle with a spoon. Crack 1 or 2 eggs into the hole and sprinkle the last ¼ cup (30 g) of cheddar across the top. Put the skillet back in the oven for 7 to 10 minutes, or until the eggs are how you'd like them.

CHILI SEAFOOD CHOWDER

Clam chowder is as much a part of summers in New England as the beach and the sun. This chowder is made with cod, but it will work with any seafood you want to throw in. The chili powder gives it a bayou feel and a much zestier flavor than the traditional favorite.

MAKES 1 HEAPING SERVING

½ cup (120 g) unsalted butter

¼ cup (31 g) all-purpose flour

½ cup (120 ml) cream (or milk in a pinch)

4 oz (115 g) cod fillet, cut into small chunks

1 carrot, peeled and diced

1 white onion, diced

1 potato, peeled and diced

1 tbsp (8 g) chili powder

1 tsp (5 g) salt

1 tsp (2 g) black pepper

1 cup (240 ml) water, plus more as needed

¼ cup (10 g) chopped fresh flat-leaf parsley

Melt the butter in a medium-size saucepan over medium-high heat. Add the flour, a few pinches at a time, stirring the whole time, until you have a paste. If you don't keep stirring your butter and flour mix will burn and your chowder will taste like it came off the grill! Add the cream and cook, stirring, until there are no lumps and the mix is soupy. I know it's tedious, but if you leave lumps, you'll end up with a floury tasting chowder and, even worse, chunks that are not fish.

Add the fish, carrot, onion, potato, chili powder, salt and pepper. Reduce the heat to medium-low and stir in the water. Cook, uncovered, until the potatoes and carrots are tender, stirring every few minutes so the chowder doesn't burn on the bottom, about 30 to 35 minutes. Add more water, 1 teaspoon (5 ml) at time, as the chowder thickens; this will prevent burning, too. When the vegetables are done, the stew is ready. Top with some parsley and eat.

MARSALA PILAF

Chicken marsala is tangy and sweet, and turning it into a pilaf makes it a filling meal that is easy to dish. Cooking the rice with a sauce instead of with water makes it really flavorful and gives it a sticky texture. As an added bonus, the tender, juicy chicken makes the rice a real meal!

MAKES 1 SERVING

1 (6–8-oz [170–230-g]) boneless chicken breast half, cut into small chunks

½ cup (62 g) all-purpose flour

¼ cup (60 ml) olive oil

¼ cup (15 g) mushrooms

¼ cup (10 g) finely chopped fresh flat-leaf parsley

2 tbsp (30 g) unsalted butter

2 tbsp (30 ml) marsala wine

Pinch of salt

Pinch of cracked black pepper

1½ cups (180 ml) chicken broth

2 razor-thin slices prosciutto, chopped fine

1 cup (210 g) rice (I like jasmine)

First toss the chicken in the flour. Then heat the olive oil in a medium-size frying pan over medium-high heat. Add the chicken and cook for about 3 to 5 minutes until browned, moving it around with a wooden spoon to keep it from burning. Add the mushrooms, parsley and butter and cook for 2–3 minutes, stirring so everything cooks evenly and doesn't burn.

Add the marsala wine, salt, pepper, chicken broth and prosciutto. Mix it all up and stir in the rice. Bring the chicken stock to a simmer, reduce the heat to low and cover pan. Don't stir, just let it cook for 20 to 25 minutes, or until all liquid is gone and the rice is soft enough to eat. That's it!

MEDITERRANEAN BAKED CHICKEN

There is so much flavor in wholesome foods like olives, peppers and onions that when you cook with them, you can make it simple. This juicy chicken has a fresh taste—it's not greasy or heavily seasoned. The recipe is very hands off and will come out perfect every time.

MAKES 1 SERVING

1 tsp (5 ml) olive oil

1 tbsp (15 ml) balsamic vinegar

1 (6–8-oz [170–230-g]) boneless chicken breast half

¼ cup (45 g) kalamata olives

½ roasted red pepper from a jar, drained and chopped

½ white onion, cut into rings

Pinch of salt

Pinch of black pepper

1 tbsp (11 g) grated Parmesan cheese

Preheat the oven to 375°F (191°C).

In a cast-iron skillet or other ovenproof pan, stir the olive oil and balsamic together. Toss the chicken with the mix to coat. Add the olives, pepper and onion to the pan and toss in the oil and vinegar. Season the chicken and veggies with the salt and pepper and sprinkle the Parmesan on top.

Put the pan in the oven, uncovered, and bake for 25 to 30 minutes, or until the chicken is cooked all the way through (cut it open to make sure). You're good to eat. You can even eat out of the cast-iron skillet if you put it on a heat-proof surface, so you only have a pot and a fork to wash.

NO-BOIL SAUSAGE AND THREE-CHEESE LASAGNA

Boiling water annoys the hell out of me, and I also hate working with limp noodles (I know what I said . . .). This recipe is easy; it makes a great meal and it uses only one pan and one bowl, so your dishwasher won't be overworked. Hot or sweet Italian sausage adds a ton of delicious grease and salt to the classic combo of sauce and cheese.

MAKES 2 LARGE SERVINGS

1 tsp (5 ml) olive oil

4 oz (115 g) loose Italian sausage meat

2 cups (475 ml) traditional tomato sauce

2 tbsp (23 g) grated Parmesan cheese

1 tsp (5 g) salt

4 oz (115 g) no-boil lasagna noodles

1 cup (230 g) ricotta cheese

1 cup (112 g) shredded mozzarella

Preheat the oven to 375°F (191°C).

Heat the olive oil in a cast-iron skillet or another ovenproof frying pan over medium-high heat. Add the sausage and cook, breaking up the meat as it browns with a wooden spoon, for about 8–10 minutes. Add the tomato sauce, grated Parm and salt. Transfer the sauce to a medium-size bowl.

Break up the lasagna noodles and layer a third of them in the bottom of the skillet. Layer a third of the ricotta on top, using a plastic spatula to smooth it out. Cover with a third of the mozzarella and a third of the sauce. Repeat the layers 2 more times and you're good to go.

Put the skillet straight into the oven and bake for 45 minutes, checking the noodles every 10 minutes or so afterwards. Once the noodles have softened and can be easily cut with a fork, your lasagna is ready to chow down.

CRUSTLESS CHICKEN POT PIE

With this recipe in your arsenal, you can get all the flavors and textures of a delicious chicken pot pie, plus some creamy beans and zesty chiles, without having to make a crust or bake it off. You basically throw these tasty ingredients into a pan and let it cook itself. Omit or add any ingredients you want.

MAKES 2 SERVINGS

3 tbsp (45 ml) olive oil

2 tomatillos, finely chopped

½ can green chiles

1 vine-ripe tomato, diced

½ white onion, chopped fine

Pinch of salt

Pinch of black pepper

1 (6–8-oz [170–230-g]) boneless chicken breast half, cut into small chunks

1 cup (254 g) canned cannellini beans

1 carrot, peeled and sliced thin

½ (12 oz [350 g]) can corn

½ cup (120 ml) chicken broth

Heat 1 tablespoon (15 ml) of the oil in a large saucepan over medium heat. Add the tomatillos, green chiles, tomato, onions, salt and pepper. Cook, stirring occasionally, until the onions have started to brown. Add the chicken, mixing it in with a wooden spoon, and cook, stirring, so nothing burns, until the chicken starts to brown.

Add the beans, carrot, corn and chicken broth and let the broth cook down for 15 to 20 minutes, stirring every 2 to 3 minutes to keep the mix from burning.

Serve by ladling into bowls and eat it like stew!

SIZZLING SKILLET STEAK AND TWICE (SORT OF) BAKED POTATO

This recipe is a quick and foolproof way to make a juicy rare steak and a loaded baked potato—the quintessential man meal. Microwaving the potato will keep the tater from drying out and cut the cooking time way down. The cheesy potato will be plenty rich on its own. My advice? Opt for the sour cream on top!

MAKES 1 SERVING

1 medium-size russet potato

1 strip bacon (optional)

2 tsp (10 g) salt

2 tsp (4 g) black pepper

½ cup (60 g) shredded cheddar

1 tsp (3 g) granulated garlic

¼ cup (60 g) unsalted butter, melted

2 tbsp (30 ml) sour cream (optional)

1 (8-oz [230-g]) shoulder steak

1 tbsp (15 ml) olive oil

Place a cast-iron skillet under the broiler and preheat the broiler.

Wash the potato and put it in a food-safe plastic shopping bag—the type you get at the grocery store—and tie the bag closed. Microwave the potato on high power until tender, about 8 minutes. Remove it from the bag carefully and set aside until it's cool enough to handle. If you are using bacon, now is a good time to crisp it up. Put the bacon strip in a frying pan over high heat and cook, flipping it once, until crispy on both sides. Drain on a paper towel to blot the grease.

Cut the potato in half lengthwise and use a spoon to take out most of the flesh, leaving the potato shell intact. Put the potato flesh in a mixing bowl and add 1 teaspoon (5 g) of the salt, 1 teaspoon (2 g) of the black pepper, the cheese, garlic and butter. Crumble in the bacon if using. Mix up everything pretty well with a fork and stuff the filling back into the potato shells. Put the potato halves on a greased baking pan (use a cooking spray like Pam; it's cool) and put them under the broiler. Broil until the cheese is completely melted and the potato skin is crispy, about 15 to 20 minutes. Remove from the oven and top with sour cream if you like.

It's important to note that this way of searing a steak is going to give you a great rare steak, but if that's not your thing, you can pop it under the broiler afterward. All I need is a fork and directions to the barn, so it works out great for me.

In a shallow bowl, toss the steak with the olive oil and season with the remaining 1 teaspoon (5 g) of salt and 1 teaspoon (2 g) of black pepper. Use oven mitts to carefully pull the cast-iron skillet out of the oven and place it on a heat-proof surface, like the top of your stove. Quickly put the steak in the skillet, making sure to include the leftover olive oil with it. Let the steak sear on one side for 1 to 1½ minutes and then turn it and sear the other side. If, after you cut into it, you decide you want it more cooked than that, put it under the broiler, cast-iron skillet and all, and broil until it's done enough for you.

Put the steak and potato on a plate and grub!

ITALIAN CHILI

Bolognese is usually considered a complicated pasta sauce, but when you boil it down—pun intended—it's actually just a mirepoix (a fancy way of saying diced carrots, celery and onions), cream, red wine and meat loaf mix. I love bolognese so much, I eat the sauce on its own a lot of times. And it finally occurred to me—it's basically Italian chili! So I added a few chili ingredients and even some Italian beans and now it's a heartier and more stand-alone version of my personal favorite. Wanna serve it over pasta? Do your thing, big guy! Note that most grocery stores sell meat loaf mix, which is a huge help for recipes like this.

MAKES 2 LARGE SERVINGS

2 tbsp (30 ml) olive oil

½ cup (70 g) diced carrots

½ cup (76 g) diced white onion

½ cup (70 g) diced celery

1 lb (455 g) meat loaf mix (veal, pork, beef)

4 vine-ripe tomatoes, diced

2 tbsp (30 ml) red wine

2 tbsp (30 ml) cream

1 chile pepper, diced

½ cup (128 g) canned black beans

½ cup (128 g) canned cannellini beans

1 tsp (4 g) sugar

1 tsp (3 g) granulated garlic

1 tbsp (8 g) chili powder

1 tsp (5 g) salt

1 tsp (2 g) black pepper

Heat the olive oil in a large saucepan over medium-high heat. Add the carrots, onion and celery. Cook, moving the veggies around with a wooden spoon, until the onions are clear, about 4–5 minutes. Add the meat loaf mix and cook, breaking the meat apart with your wooden spoon as it begins to brown. Add the tomatoes to the pot, and turn the heat down to medium-low.

Add the rest of the ingredients, stirring once to blend well. Cover and simmer for 30 to 40 minutes, stirring every 5 minutes or so to keep the bottom from burning.

THIRTY-MINUTE CHILI

Chili is one of my favorite things to make—it can be cooked with almost anything and eaten in so many ways. I keep it pretty traditional, but like to get a little more flavor by using ground pork and beef, plus a few different hot peppers. If you like it hot, rock out. Heat not your thing? Skip the habanero and dial it back, dude.

MAKES 2 SERVINGS

1 tsp (5 ml) olive oil

½ medium-size white onion, minced (chopped as fine as possible)

4 oz (115 g) ground beef (80/20)

4 oz (115 g) ground pork

2 vine-ripe beefsteak tomatoes, chopped fine

1 (16-oz [455-g]) can chili beans, with their liquid

½ jalapeño pepper

1 bell pepper

¼ habanero pepper

½ chile pepper

1 tbsp (15 g) salt

1 tsp (2 g) black pepper

1 tbsp (6 g) sweet paprika

1 tbsp (15 ml) sour cream (optional)

¼ cup (30 g) shredded cheddar cheese (optional, sort of)

Heat the olive oil in the biggest frying pan you own over medium heat. Add the onion and cook until lightly browned, stirring with a wooden spoon so the onions don't burn, about 2 to 3 minutes. Add the ground beef and pork and cook, stirring and breaking up the meat into small chunks. Stir in the tomatoes and add the beans, liquid and all. Add the jalapeño, bell pepper, habanero and chile pepper. Finally, add the salt, black pepper and paprika and stir again.

Cover the pan, turn the heat down to medium-low and cook, stirring every few minutes. The tomatoes and beans will add a lot liquid, which you want to cook down (meaning you want the chili to thicken up, man). Once the chili is as thick as you like it, bang—you're ready to pull it off the stove.

Put half of the chili into a bowl (the other half is leftovers or an ingredient in some badass mac and cheese balls [p. 99]?). Top with the sour cream and cheese if you like. Enjoy!

BROCCOLI AND CHEESE CRISPY CASSEROLE

When I was growing up, we would always spend Thanksgiving in western New York with my Mom's family, and those fine folks would make some of the simplest comfort food I've ever eaten. My favorite turkey-day side dish was broccoli casserole, which I have tweaked over the years to include fresh ingredients and a panko topping. Any vegetable that can be made into a comfort food is a win in my book. This dish is a kick-ass replacement for mashed potatoes.

MAKES 2 SERVINGS

4 cups (950 ml) water
1 lb (455 g) broccoli
½ cup (60 g) diced Velveeta cheese
¼ cup (60 g) unsalted butter
¼ cup (60 ml) milk
1 tsp (5 g) salt
1 tsp (2 g) black pepper
1 cup (54 g) panko bread crumbs

Preheat the oven to 350°F (177°C).

Fill a large pot with the water, and bring to a boil over high heat. Add the broccoli and boil until it's soft enough to break up with a fork, about 12–15 minutes. Drain and return the broccoli to the pot. Turn the heat down to medium and add the cheese, half of the butter, the milk, salt and pepper. Cook, stirring, until the cheese is completely melted and blended with the broccoli.

Melt the rest of the butter in a bowl in the microwave and stir in the bread crumbs. Pour the cheese and broccoli into a baking pan and spread the topping over the mix. Put the baking pan into the oven for about 45 minutes.

PERFECT HERB CHICKEN AND SALTY POTATO PUREE

Roasting chicken is an easy process, and it doesn't require much thought to give it a ton of flavor. Set the chicken up in a brine the night before, dry it out the next the day in the fridge, and when you come home from work, roast it. Although the first two steps might seem unnecessary, your chicken will be so crisp and flavorful this way! The salty potatoes are a great touch and are based on a simple recipe my uncle Dave made famous in Little Valley, New York, where he sold barbecue at the county fair.

MAKES 1 SERVING

BRINE

4 cups (950 ml) water
2 tbsp (43 g) honey
2 tbsp (24 g) sugar
2 tbsp (30 g) salt
¼ cup (10 g) fresh rosemary

2 chicken thighs, skin on
4 cups (950 ml) water
¼ cup (60 g) kosher salt
2 cups (360 g) baby red potatoes
¼ cup (60 g) unsalted butter
Pinch of cracked pepper
Honey for drizzling (optional)
Finely chopped fresh flat-leaf parsley for sprinkling (optional)

In a small saucepan, combine the water, honey, sugar, salt and rosemary. Bring to a boil over high heat, lower the heat to medium, and simmer for 5 minutes. Refrigerate for 1 hour, or until cool.

Put the chicken into a zipper-top bag and add the brine. Shake them up and refrigerate for at least 8 hours.

Remove the chicken from the bag and place it on a rack in a roasting pan, and put it in the fridge. Leave it there for another 8 hours or so, uncovered. Toss the brine in the trash.

Preheat the oven to 400°F (204°C). Put the chicken thighs on a baking sheet or in a cast-iron skillet, skin-side up, and roast for 10 minutes. Lower the heat to 375°F (191°C) and cook for another 25 to 30 minutes. If you have an instant-read thermometer, the chicken is done when it registers 165°F (74°C). Or cutting into the chicken works, too.

While the chicken is roasting, pour the 4 cups (950 ml) of water into a medium-size pot and bring to a boil over high heat. Add the kosher salt and potatoes. Boil for 25 minutes or until the potatoes are soft enough so that a fork goes through easily. Drain the potatoes. While they're still hot, put them in a blender or food processor with the butter and black pepper. Blend until the potatoes are smooth.

Spoon the potatoes onto a plate, smoothing them out in a circular motion with a spoon. Place the chicken thighs on top of the potatoes. If you're feeling fancy, drizzle a little honey over the top and sprinkle with parsley.

BURGER BOMB BREAD PUDDING

The trick to a good bread pudding is mixing everything up really well and making sure that when you bake it, you let the whole thing firm up. Otherwise you'll be eating a soggy mess. By starting with a can't-miss combo of greasy meat, fresh bomb mix and melted cheese, you guarantee that this bread pudding will be a great meal or a few terrific snacks.

MAKES 1 SERVING

¼ cup (60 ml) olive oil

½ medium white onion, chopped

1 yellow bell pepper

½ cup (30 g) white mushrooms, chopped

8 oz (230 g) ground beef

3 eggs

½ cup (120 ml) milk

1 tsp (5 g) salt

4 croissants (any bread will work)

1 cup (120 g) shredded cheddar cheese

Preheat your oven to 375°F (191°C).

Heat the olive oil in a large frying pan over medium-high heat. Add the vegetables and cook, moving them around the pan with a wooden spoon—sautéing them, if you will. Once the veggies seem to be getting soft, in a few minutes, add the ground beef. Cook, continuing to stir with a wooden spoon so the ground beef breaks apart and becomes well browned. In about 5 minutes the ground beef should be well browned, and you're ready to move on. Keep in mind, you don't want raw ground beef in your mix but if it's a little undercooked that's OK because it's all getting baked.

Crack the eggs into a small bowl, add the milk and salt, and stir it until the mix is smooth and the egg is completely broken up. Remember: nobody likes shells in their bread pudding. Cut your croissants into smallish pieces; it doesn't have to be fancy or exact. Put them in a larger bowl and add the meat and veggie mixture with a slotted spoon, so the pan juices are mostly left behind. Stir this all up, letting the bread absorb the juices that made it in. Add the egg mixture and the cheese and again mix it all up. I find that clean hands make the best mixing tool for something like this.

Put the mix into a baking pan, cupcake tin, cast-iron skillet, pie dish—anything it will fit into that you're sure is ovenproof. Place in the hot oven and set a timer for 20 minutes. Check to see that the center of the pudding is firm. If it isn't, check back every few minutes until it is. Once the whole pudding is firm to the touch and no liquid is visible on the surface, pull it out and dig in!

BACON AND PARM ROASTED VEGGIE MEDLEY

Weekday nights have always been tough for me. Getting home from work and wanting a quality meal without the bother of cooking something time-consuming is a tall order. This really basic roasted veggies recipe is one solution to the problem. You feel like you're eating a real meal without having to do very much. The raw bacon will season the veggies and the high heat keeps them from getting soggy.

MAKES 1 SERVING

1 medium-size zucchini

1 medium-size yellow squash

1 vine-ripe tomato

2 strips bacon

1 tbsp (15 ml) olive oil

1 tsp (2 g) cracked black pepper

1 clove garlic, minced

¼ cup (45 g) grated Parmesan cheese

Preheat the oven to 425°F (218°C).

Cut the zucchini and yellow squash in half lengthwise. You're only going to use half of each one for this recipe. (Put the other 2 halves in the fridge to save for another use.) Cut the zucchini and yellow squash halves crosswise, and then cut each quarter lengthwise into ½-inch (13-mm) strips. Cut the tomato in half, from the stem end to the bottom. Cut each half into ¼-inch (6-mm-) thick half-moons. Cut the bacon strips into small pieces.

In a medium-size bowl, toss the veggies, bacon, olive oil, pepper and minced garlic. Spread out the mix on a baking sheet and sprinkle the Parm over the top. Roast for about 10 to 15 minutes, depending on how you like them. I like mine pretty crispy, so 15 does it for me.

SPICY PEANUT BUTTER BEEF

Melting a little peanut butter in a pan with meat fat and spicy pepper flakes makes for a really easy Asian-inspired dish that comes together fast. The peanut butter is creamy and will coat the noodles for a great sauce, while the sesame oil adds to the nuttiness of the recipe. If you don't want the heat, just skip the flakes. And the same can be said of any of the veggies. Fresh veggies are a plus, but I figured I'd save you the cutting job for a change.

MAKES 1 LARGE SERVING

3 oz (85 g) udon noodles

1 tsp (5 ml) sesame oil

1 (8-oz [230-g]) shoulder steak, cut into thin strips

1 tbsp (11 g) peanut butter

1 tsp (2 g) red pepper flakes

8 oz (225 g) frozen Asian vegetables

Salt to taste

Fill a large pot with water, and bring to a boil over high heat. Cook the noodles according to the package directions until tender. Drain them really well and set them aside to dry a little.

Coat a large frying pan with the sesame oil and place it on medium heat. Add the steak and cook, stirring constantly, until cooked through, in about 5 minutes. As the steak cooks, slowly stir in the peanut butter until it blends with the steak juices and oil. Next mix in the pepper flakes. When the steak is done, take it out of the pan, scraping out the sauce with it, and transfer to a bowl.

Return the pan to medium heat and put in the frozen veggies. Let the veggies thaw out for 3 or 4 minutes and then turn the heat up to high and cook, stirring constantly. Once all the liquid has evaporated, return the meat and sauce to the pan and stir rapidly to warm them. Add the noodles and stir for 30 seconds more. Season with salt and dig in.

GAME DAY

CHAPTER THREE

GRUB

FANTASTIC PIG-OUT FOOD

The recipes that are the most fun to share with other guys are definitely the junk food. It will come as no surprise that the recipes I love the most are almost always stuff that my wife and her friends would never even touch, like the Short Rib and Potato Slaw on Toast (p. 80) or the Puff Pastry Pizza (p. 75). But my buddies and I scarf them down when we're having a few beers or watching a Pats game. Herb and Romano Hot Wings (p. 83) or Hot Honey Chicken Skewers (p. 84), Buffalo Chicken Queso (p. 79) or Chubby Chickpea Hummus (p. 91)—there's a snack for any mood you might be in. The idea behind these recipes is simple—don't worry about whether they're good for you; just add more cheese or sauce and go to town!

PUFF PASTRY PIZZA

This is an awesome way to make a few pies if you've got buddies coming over for the game. Puff pastry makes for an even better snack food, if you can believe it, than regular pizza dough, and this is so easy that you can try out all kinds of crazy combos. My fave is buffalo chicken and bacon, courtesy of my boy Matt, who first suggested it to me.

MAKES 3 SERVINGS

1 (10-x-20-in [25-x-50-cm]) puff pastry sheet

1 cup (240 ml) traditional tomato sauce

1 tbsp (3 g) dried basil

1½ cups (167 g) shredded mozzarella cheese

½ white onion, cut into rings

½ cup (62 g) chopped cooked chicken breast (Rotisserie chicken is good)

1 tbsp (15 ml) hot sauce, such as Frank's RedHot

½ cup (60 g) cooked bacon

¼ cup (34 g) crumbled blue cheese

1 tsp (2 g) red pepper flakes (optional)

Preheat the oven to 350°F (177°C).

Put the puff pastry sheet on a baking sheet that is big enough to contain it and let it thaw for 10 minutes. Spread the tomato sauce evenly across the sheet, leaving a 1-inch (2.5-cm) border on all sides without sauce. Sprinkle the basil over the whole sheet next. Do the same with the mozzarella cheese and then scatter the onion on top.

Toss the chicken with the hot sauce in a small bowl and scatter it around the whole pizza, along with any sauce left in the bowl if you like. Finish up by sprinkling the bacon and blue cheese over the pizza.

Pop the pie in the oven for about 25 minutes, or until the puff pastry has puffed up and the cheeses have browned. Take the pizza out of the oven and let it cool for 5 to 10 minutes. This isn't a regular pizza crust, and eating it right out of the oven will be very messy! Top with red pepper flakes (if using).

Cut the pie into squares and serve at room temperature.

THE BEST FRIGGIN' BURGER EVER

For years now I've been avoiding making burgers when my boys come over for a BBQ for one simple reason—they're *boring*, and I hate boring food. Sure, you can dress a burger up to make it look sexy, but all the excitement is lost when we know what plain Jane burger is under the dress. This past year it hit me: I don't use 100 percent beef to make meatballs or meat sauce, so why use all beef for a burger? And here it is, a burger that's really hard to dry out, has awesome flavor and, when covered in makeup and avocado, has you dying to get it in its birthday suit!

MAKES 8 SERVINGS

1½ lb (680 g) ground beef (I like 80/20)

1½ lb (680 g) hot Italian sausage, removed from the casings

2 eggs

½ cup (60 g) dry unseasoned bread crumbs

1 tsp (5 g) salt

1 tsp (2 g) black pepper

1 tsp (3 g) granulated garlic

8 slices Swiss cheese (optional)

¼ cup (60 ml) vegetable oil if using a frying pan instead of a grill

FOR SERVING (OPTIONAL)

2 ripe avocados, sliced

Strips of cooked bacon (optional)

1 white onion, separated into rings

1 vine-ripe tomato, sliced

8 Boston or Bibb lettuce leaves

½ cup (110 ml) Cajun mayo (optional)

8 of your favorite bakery-fresh rolls

Cover 1 full-size baking sheet (18 x 26 in [46 x 66 cm]) or 2 smaller ones with wax paper. In a large bowl mix the ground beef and the Italian sausage with your hands until they are one meaty mess. Crack in the eggs (no shells!), add the bread crumbs, salt, pepper and garlic and mix again with your hands until everything is well blended. Make 8 equal balls and place them on the wax paper. No wax paper? Just put the burgers on the baking sheet and wash up later, man. Press the burgers down until they are about ½ inch (13 mm) thick.

Fire up the grill to medium heat. Place the burgers on the grill and close the lid. After about 3 minutes, flip the burgers and cover again. Repeat until the burgers reach 155°F (68°C) on an instant-read thermometer, or until they're cooked through (remember there's pork—so no medium-rare). If you're adding cheese, when the burgers are just a little underdone (for the scientists in the room, 145°F [63°C]), put a piece of cheese on each burger and close the lid. The cheese should melt pretty quickly, so check on it once per minute.

Don't have a grill, or it's pouring out? Take the biggest frying pan you have, and heat the oil in it on medium heat. Place as many burgers as you can in the pan without crowding them. (Hint, if the answer is 1 burger, you might think about getting a bigger pan, bro.) Put a lid on the pan and cook for about 2 minutes, then flip the burgers and repeat. Just like grilling, you're going to repeat this step until the burgers are done, adding the cheese, if using, when they're a little underdone.

Obviously with a burger, variety is the spice of life. Dress your burgers however you like. In addition to the Swiss cheese, I like avocado, bacon, white onion, tomato and a leaf of Boston lettuce on mine. Condiments? I rock with Cajun mayo.

BUFFALO CHICKEN QUESO

Nothing gets a guys-only party started like buffalo chicken, and this recipe adds melted cheese, so you can dip tortilla chips into it. As a dip, it's easy and awesome. Go overboard and make some extra; you can use it in Buffalo Chicken Huevos Rancheros (p. 129) if you don't finish it all!

MAKES 1 SERVING

1 tbsp (15 ml) canola oil

1 (6–8-oz [170–230-g]) boneless chicken breast half, chopped

½ white onion, diced fine

1 tsp (5 g) unsalted butter

2 tsp (10 ml) Frank's RedHot buffalo wings sauce

1 cup (56 g) shredded pepper Jack cheese

½ cup (60 g) shredded cheddar cheese

Pinch of black pepper

Preheat the broiler.

Heat the canola oil in a cast-iron skillet or another ovenproof frying pan over medium heat. Add the chopped chicken and diced white onion, and cook, stirring the chicken and onion with a wooden spoon so they don't burn, until the chicken is browned, in 3 to 5 minutes. Add the butter and hot sauce, mix it all up, and cook for 1 minute or until the butter melts. Mix it up and take it off the heat.

Add the cheeses and black pepper to the skillet and mix it all up. Put the skillet in the oven and bake until the cheese melts completely, in about 5 minutes. But keep an eye on it since not every oven cooks the same. You want the cheese browned a little on top and melted all the way, but not burnt or crispy!

SHORT RIBS AND POTATO SLAW ON TOAST

I definitely consider myself a meat and potatoes kind of guy, so in the spirit of finding innovative ways to enjoy old favorites, I created this recipe. It makes a great snack to stuff your face with, but it could also be served in bigger portions for a meal.

MAKES 6 TOASTS

½ cup (120 ml) canola oil

2 (6-oz [170-g]) beef short ribs

2 tsp (10 g) salt

2 tsp (4 g) black pepper

1 tsp (2 g) paprika

1 medium potato

1 medium white onion

½ cup (120 ml) water

1 loaf French bread

6 tsp (30 ml) Cajun mayo

6 slices pepper Jack cheese

Heat ¼ cup (60 ml) of the oil in a large frying pan over medium heat. While the oil is heating, season the short ribs evenly with 1 teaspoon (5 g) of the salt, 1 teaspoon (2 g) of the pepper and the paprika. Put the short ribs in the oil; they should sizzle as soon as they're in (if they don't, the oil isn't hot enough yet). After about 3 minutes, turn the ribs and brown on the other side. I get it, standing over a hot frying pan isn't your idea of fun. But burning the short ribs won't be either, and that brown crust you're seeing? That's all the flavor, man! Remove the ribs from the pan and set aside.

Wash the potato and peel the onion. Leaving the skin on the tater, cut very thin slices (as thin as you can). Do the same with the onion slices. In the same pan that you used for the short ribs, heat the remaining ¼ cup (60 ml) of oil over high heat. Slide the onion and potato slices into the oil and season with the remaining 1 teaspoon (5 g) of salt and 1 teaspoon (2 g) of pepper. Cook, stirring often—these will burn quicker than the ribs—for about 2 to 3 minutes, or until brown.

Return the ribs to the pan, reduce the heat to medium and add ¼ cup (60 ml) of water. Cook, checking the pan every few minutes to make sure the water has not cooked off completely (if it gets close, add the remaining ¼ cup [60 ml] of water). After about 10 minutes, check the temperature of the meat with an instant-read thermometer. Once the ribs have reached 155°F (68°C), or when you cut into the center and they're cooked the way you like them, remove the ribs from the pan and set aside to rest.

Preheat the oven to 350°F (177°C).

Cut six ¼-inch-(6-mm-) thick slices of the French bread. (Save the rest for another use.) Spread 1 teaspoon (5 ml) of Cajun mayo on each slice. Slice 6 equal portions of the meat (they don't have to be neat, even slices) and place them on the bread. Top each toast with an equal portion of the potato and onion, and cover with a slice of cheese. Put the bread with its toppings on a baking sheet and bake for 6 minutes, or until the cheese is melted. Now eat!

NOTE: If you don't have Cajun mayo, mix 1 teaspoon (5 g) Cajun seasoning with 6 teaspoons (35 ml) mayo.

HERB AND ROMANO HOT WINGS

My mom grew up an hour west of Buffalo, and we actually lived there for a few years when I was little. One thing I never miss when I'm there is the opportunity to grab a few hot wings at a dive bar or three—their flavor is so different there than it is anywhere else. These wings are a lot easier to make and much better for you. But they pack a similar amount of heat, and the cheesy herb seasoning makes them an awesome game-time decision.

MAKES ABOUT 20 WINGS

½ cup (115 g) unsalted butter
2 cloves garlic, minced
½ cup (90 g) grated Parmesan cheese
1 tsp (2 g) cracked black pepper
Pinch of salt
Pinch of cayenne pepper
¼ cup (10 g) chopped fresh rosemary
2 lb (910 g) chicken wings

Preheat the oven to 450°F (232°C).

Melt the butter in a large frying pan over medium-high heat. Throw the garlic in and let that beautiful smell fill your whole place. (It's too bad no one is coming over right about now because he'd swear you were the best chef he knows!) Cook, stirring the garlic with a wooden spoon for 1 or 2 minutes, and turn off the heat.

In a zipper-top plastic bag, mix the remaining ingredients, except for the wings. Pour your garlic butter into another zipper-top plastic bag, and add the wings, tossing them in the butter. Now put the butter-coated wings into the bag with the cheese and seasonings, and shake them around a bunch, like a Shake 'n Bake commercial.

With clean hands, take the wings out of the bag and put them on a baking sheet. Put the baking sheet in the oven (after washing your hands again, man, come on!) and bake for 40 minutes. Check on them every 10 minutes after they've been in for a while, just to make sure they aren't burning, but let them get crispy. An instant-read thermometer would help here (it should register 165°F [74°C]) but if they're crispy on the outside, they'll be juicy inside.

HOT HONEY CHICKEN SKEWERS

The summer I turned 21, I used to go to a bar after work with my buddies and eat chicken wings 'til I was ready to puke. One of my favorite flavors was this hot honey sauce with red pepper flakes in it. I make a similar sauce for skewers, using pineapple and just a little honey to bring the same sweetness. It's a fresh take on fried wings, which goes great with rice.

MAKES 2 SKEWERS

1 tbsp (15 g) unsalted butter
1 tbsp (21 ml) honey
1 tsp (2 g) red pepper flakes
½ cup (120 ml) water
1 (8-oz [230-g]) boneless chicken breast half
1 red bell pepper
½ white onion
1 tsp (5 g) salt
8 chunks canned pineapple

Preheat the oven to 400°F (204°C). If you're using wooden skewers, soak them in water for at least 30 minutes.

Melt the butter in a small saucepan over low heat and add the honey. Stir in the red pepper flakes and add the water. Allow to simmer for 10 minutes, stirring often so the mix doesn't burn as it cooks down to a syrup.

Cut the chicken breast into 8 equal chunks. Cut the sides off the red pepper and cut them into 8 pieces also. Cut the onion into 8 chunks, each with 3 to 4 layers of onion.

When your sauce is ready, salt the chicken and put it in the sauce, along with the peppers. Make sure they're completely coated, and then pull them out. Thread a skewer with 1 piece each of the chicken, pepper, pineapple and onion, in any order you like. Repeat 3 more times, so the skewer has 4 pieces of each ingredient. Do the same thing with the second skewer.

Put the skewers on a baking sheet sprayed with nonstick cooking spray, and put them in the oven. Cook for 20 to 25 minutes, turning them halfway through. Cut into a couple of chicken pieces to make sure they're fully cooked and grub!

FALAFEL

These crispy Middle Eastern chickpea balls are light, somewhat healthful and definitely a great game-day snack. They take a little bit of work, but they're worth it. And the mix can be kept in the freezer for a quick-and-easy sandwich or snack. Serve with the tahini sauce and hummus.

MAKES 12 TO 15 FALAFEL BALLS

TAHINI SAUCE (OPTIONAL)

1 tbsp (15 ml) tahini (sesame paste)
2 tbsp (30 ml) water
Pinch of salt
Pinch of granulated garlic
1 tsp (5 ml) fresh lemon juice

FALAFEL

1 cup (201 g) dried chickpeas
1 cup (40 g) fresh flat-leaf parsley, roughly chopped
1 tsp (3 g) granulated garlic
1 tsp (2 g) ground cumin
Pinch of ground coriander
1 tsp (5 g) salt
Pinch of black pepper
2 cups (475 ml) canola oil
Hummus for serving, homemade (p. 91) or store-bought

MAKING THE TAHINI SAUCE

Combine the ingredients in a blender and blend until smooth. That's tahini sauce! Pour into a bowl and set aside while you make the falafel.

MAKING THE FALAFEL

Wash off the chickpeas to get rid of any dirt or gunk on them and put them in a medium-size bowl. Cover the chickpeas with at least 1 inch (2.5 cm) of the hottest water your sink will run (somewhere around 110°F [43°C]). Let the chickpeas sit for 1 hour or so. They should double in size.

If you have a meat grinder, this is the time to use it. If you don't, grab a food processor or blender. Feed the chickpeas and parsley through the meat grinder together and into a bowl. If you're using a food processor or blender, make sure to pulse the chickpeas, turning the machine on and off every few seconds to get a ground-up batter. Transfer to a bowl and add the garlic, cumin, coriander, salt and pepper.

Heat the oil in a large frying pan or saucepan over medium heat until a pinch of falafel batter sizzles as soon as its dropped in. Shape the falafel balls with your hands, dipping your fingers in water to keep the batter from sticking to them. Pack them well, but don't squeeze them too tight, or they'll be dense. Put them in the oil and cook for 2 to 3 minutes, depending on how large you made them. If they aren't fully covered in oil, flip them after 1 minute. Serve them with hummus and the tahini sauce, if you've made it.

STUFFED CHERRY PEPPERS

For a light snack I like to stuff peppers with all kinds of different stuff. This recipe has a really basic Mediterranean mix with a little bit of honey for a change of pace. The peppers and honey make a sweetness that complements the grease of the cheese and meat really nicely.

MAKES 8 STUFFED PEPPERS

8 two-bite cherry peppers
8 (2-inch [5-cm]) sweet peppers
½ roasted red pepper from a jar, drained
8 razor-thin slices mozzarella cheese
8 razor-thin slices prosciutto
1 tbsp (21 ml) honey

Preheat the oven to 375°F (191°C).

Cut the tops off each of the cherry peppers, and clean the insides out. Chop up the sweet and roasted peppers, cheese and prosciutto and mix them together really well in a small bowl. Stir in the honey.

Stuff the cherry peppers so they're as full as possible and put them on a baking sheet. Put the baking sheet in the oven and cook the peppers for 15 to 20 minutes, or until the cheese oozes. Your peppers are ready to be eaten!

CHUBBY CHICKPEA HUMMUS

Hummus has quickly become America's favorite game-time dip. In fact, last year it was the Super Bowl's official dip. Why not? It's creamy and smooth and has a really great garlicky flavor. Stir in some hot sauce or Cajun seasoning to kick it up.

MAKES 2 SERVINGS

4 cups (945 ml) water
2 cups (508 g) canned chickpeas, rinsed
¼ cup (60 ml) olive oil
2 tbsp (30 ml) tahini paste
1 tsp (3 g) granulated garlic
Pinch of salt
1 tsp (5 ml) fresh lemon juice
1 tsp (5 ml) olive oil
Pinch of paprika (optional)
Crackers or bread for serving (optional)

In a small saucepan, bring the water to a boil over high heat. Add the chickpeas and boil for 20 minutes. Once the chickpeas easily mush in your hand, they're ready for hummus!

In a food processor or in a blender on high speed, mix the chickpeas (still hot), the ¼ cup (60 ml) oil, the tahini, garlic, salt and lemon juice. Add a few drops of water at a time to help it all blend. Process or blend until creamy and smooth, which may take as long as 4 minutes.

Put the hummus on a plate and if you want, drizzle with the 1 teaspoon (5 ml) of olive oil and sprinkle with paprika. Eat with your favorite crackers, bread or fingers.

GORGONZOLA POTATO SALAD

This might be my favorite recipe, because it's easy and has the flavors and textures I love—tangy crunch from apples and salty cheesiness from the gorgonzola. I created this while getting ready for a BBQ and was feeling bored with my usual potato salad. My buddy Mark will argue it's not as good as his potato salad, which he mixes with equal parts mayo and arm hair, but you'll have to judge for yourself!

MAKES 2 SERVINGS

2 potatoes, skin on
1 Granny Smith apple
¼ cup (12 g) chopped scallion
½ cup (68 g) crumbled gorgonzola cheese
¼ cup (55 ml) mayo
1 tsp (5 g) salt
1 tsp (2 g) cracked black pepper

Wash the potatoes and put them in a food-safe plastic shopping bag—the type you get at the grocery store—and tie the bag closed. Microwave the potatoes on high power until you can pass the blade of a knife straight through without any real effort, about 10 to 12 minutes.

While your potatoes nuke, cut the apple into pieces about half the size of bite size. Transfer to a medium-size bowl and add the scallion, cheese, mayo, salt and pepper.

When your potatoes are ready, carefully cut them into little pieces. Even with a decent knife, you'll end up mashing them as much as cutting them—that's OK. This potato salad is almost a mashed potatoes dish. Mix the potatoes into the bowl of goodies and eat immediately.

GARLIC PARMESAN MONKEY BREAD FROM A CAN

My mom used to make monkey bread the traditional way when I was a kid, with cinnamon and sugar. I make mine with garlic and Parmesan. For a spicy treat, add some buffalo sauce to the butter mix and use blue cheese crumbles with chili powder or red pepper flakes.

4 SNACK-SIZE SERVINGS

½ cup (120 g) unsalted butter
1 cup (180 g) grated Parmesan cheese
¼ cup (34 g) garlic powder
¼ cup (10 g) chopped fresh flat-leaf parsley
1 roll of home-style biscuits

Preheat the oven to 350°F (177°C).

Put the butter into a small microwave-safe dish and microwave for 15 seconds at a time until melted. You may need to do this 2 or 3 times, but don't cut corners or you might burn the butter.

Put the Parmesan, garlic powder and parsley on a plate and use a fork to mix it all together evenly.

Open the biscuit package. Cut each biscuit into fourths or sixths. Dunk each piece in the melted butter and roll it in the dry ingredients. Drop it into a baking dish or baking pan.

After all the pieces are in the baking dish, put the dish in the oven for 15 to 20 minutes, or until the bread is fully puffed and light brown. Take it out of the oven and start pulling it apart.

THIS LITTLE PIGGY GREW UP

My buddy Mike loves food, but he eats a total of, like, six food items. One of those items is pigs in a blanket, so he's always trying to figure out ways to keep the idea fresh. This is a take on the sausages sold outside Fenway Park, turned into pigs in a blanket. Serve them with your favorite condiment—I like stone-ground mustard.

MAKES 10 SAUSAGES IN BLANKETS

2 tbsp (30 ml) oil

10 hot Italian sausages (breakfast size)

1 (10-x-20-in [25-x-50-cm]) puff pastry sheet

4 oz (115 g) pepper Jack cheese

1 green bell pepper

1 white onion, peeled

Preheat the oven to 375°F (191°C). Coat a baking sheet with nonstick cooking spray.

Heat the oil in a large frying pan over medium-high heat. Add the sausages to the pan and brown them all over, about 4 minutes total. Pull them off the heat.

Cut the puff pastry into 10 strips about the same length as the sausages. The width should be about double the circumference of a sausage. Lay out the strips on the baking sheet. Place a piece of cheese the size of the sausage on each pastry piece. Next place the sausage, and then pieces of pepper and onion the same size. Wrap the puff pastry around the sausage, overlapping the long ends only a little bit and pinch the seam closed, leaving the pastry open on both ends, like a pig in a blanket! Repeat with the remaining pastry, sausage, pepper and onion. Put the baking sheet in the oven and bake for 20 to 25 minutes, or until the puff pastry has puffed up and browned. You're ready to eat!

JALAPEÑO MAC & CHEESE BALLS

I always bust my friends' balls when it comes to making mac and cheese, since they're not all "from scratch" guys. I ask them how they make their cheese sauce. The most common response? They toss Velveeta or another melting cheese right into the hot pasta. Needless to say, that's not what I consider the best way, so buried in this easy-to-make fried mac recipe is a great cheese sauce recipe. There are lots of ways to kick this up more than a few notches—like mixing in leftover chili or buffalo chicken before frying—but this keeps it simple and kick-ass.

MAKES 4 TO 6 CHEESE BALLS

1 cup (116 g) elbow macaroni
2 tbsp (30 g) unsalted butter
¼ cup (31 g) all-purpose flour
½ cup (60 ml) milk
1 tsp (5 g) salt
1 tsp (2 g) black pepper
1 tsp (3 g) granulated garlic
½ cup (60 g) shredded cheddar cheese
½ jalapeño pepper, cut into very thin rings
1 cup (60 g) dry unseasoned bread crumbs
1 cup (235 ml) oil

This recipe calls for 2 pots, so if you own only one (or none), time to get to the store or knock on your neighbor's door.

Fill a medium-size pot with water, and bring to a boil over high heat. Cook the macaroni according to the package directions until it is tender and ready to eat. Give it one stir after about 1 minute, to keep the macaroni from sticking. Drain the macaroni and rinse with cold water to stop the cooking. Set aside.

In a second medium-size pot, melt the butter over medium-high heat, stirring with a wooden spoon to keep the butter from burning. Add a pinch of flour at a time, stirring it in until the mix becomes a paste. This step is super important: once the butter and flour have gotten pasty, immediately add milk, about 2 tablespoons (30 ml) at a time, until the mix is saucy. Repeat until the milk and the flour are both gone. Don't take a shortcut and mix it all up at once, man—and I know that was your first thought—the sauce is gonna be lumpy and gross. When you have a smooth sauce, add the salt, pepper and garlic. Stir in the shredded cheese, mixing constantly until the cheese has melted into the sauce. Turn the heat down to low and let the sauce cook for 15 minutes, stirring every few minutes. You want the sauce to be thick, not soupy, for the mac to hold.

Put the pasta into the cheese sauce (that way only one pan is a real mess), add the jalapeño pepper, and stir it in well. Let it sit until the sauce is cool enough for you to stick your hands in. As the pasta cools, the cheese sauce will get sticky and a little bit thicker. Wet your hands and start rolling the pasta into 4 to 6 equal balls. Put them on a baking sheet, or a plate, and put them in the fridge. Leave them for 30 minutes.

Put the bread crumbs into a shallow bowl. Heat the oil in a large frying pan over medium-high heat. In about 2 minutes, put a pinch of bread crumbs into the oil. If it sizzles, the oil is ready. (Don't test it with the cheese balls; they'll get soggy and oily.) Once the oil is hot, coat the mac balls completely with bread crumbs and put them into the oil. Fry for about 1 minute until browned, and roll to the other side and repeat. Once the balls are browned, remove from the pan and drain on paper. The coolest thing about cooking these? Nothing in the mix is raw or dangerous, so undercooking isn't going to make you sick.

LOBSTER BAKED ZITI

Lobster is great, especially when it's smothered in butter. What's the logical next step? Smother it in cheese and cream and toss it with pasta! This dish is fine dining meets face-stuffing comfort food in the way that lobster mac pretends to be. Note that there are a few options for getting cooked lobster meat: once a year I go down to the beach with a few buddies and we start the weekend off by cooking live lobsters. If you feel like going through the trouble of boiling and ripping through one of those mean little guys for the freshest dish possible, I applaud your efforts. But it's cool to get a frozen lobster tail and steam it just the same. If that's the route you go, follow the instructions on the package. If you live near the coast, you can buy fresh lobster meat at a fish store, but it will cost you a fortune.

MAKES 1 LARGE SERVING

2 cups (232 g) ziti
½ cup (120 g) unsalted butter
Pinch of salt
Pinch of black pepper
1 clove garlic, minced
4 oz (115 g) cooked lobster meat
¼ cup (45 g) grated Parmesan cheese
½ cup (120 ml) cream
¼ cup (28 g) shredded mozzarella

Preheat the oven to 400°F (204°C).

Fill a medium-size pot with water, and bring to a boil over high heat. Cook the ziti according to the package directions until it is tender and ready to eat. Drain well and set aside.

Melt the butter in a large frying pan over medium heat and add the salt, black pepper and garlic. Stir in the lobster meat and Parmesan cheese. Once everything is mixed up pretty well, add the cream gradually, stirring constantly until the cream sauce is well blended and smooth.

Mix the cooked ziti into the sauce, right there in the frying pan, and pour the whole thing into a cast-iron skillet or baking pan. Sprinkle the mozzarella over the top and put it into the oven. Bake for about 10 minutes or until the cheese has melted and browned, and you're good to dig in.

APPLE-WALNUT POTATO PANCAKES

When I was growing up, we'd make potato pancakes, which are called latkes, every year on the Jewish holiday of Hanukkah. We made them a whole bunch of different ways—sometimes shredded, sometimes mashed. This recipe is simple in that it just uses sliced potatoes, which create almost a fried hash brown. The apples give it a nice sweet crisp.

MAKES 1 SERVING (4 PANCAKES)

1 apple, peeled
1 potato, peeled
1 egg
1 tbsp (7 g) chopped walnuts
½ cup (62 g) all-purpose flour
1 tsp (5 g) salt
Pinch of black pepper
1 cup (235 ml) oil
Applesauce or sour cream for serving

Chop the apple into ¼-inch (6-mm) cubes. If you own a mandolin, slice the potato on the thinnest setting. If you don't have one, just cut the potato as thin as you can. Crack the egg into a medium-size bowl and beat it well. Add the walnuts, the apple and potato slices and then the flour, salt and pepper and mix them up well.

Form the mix into 4 patties—it's OK that they're not smooth. The patchwork look is one of the cool things about these pancakes.

Heat the oil in a large, deep frying pan over medium-high heat. After about 3 minutes, check to see if the oil is hot enough by sprinkling in a little flour. It should sizzle right away. Put the patties into the hot oil and flatten them out a little when they first go in. Let them fry for about 30 seconds, and then move them slightly with a wooden spoon to keep them from sticking to the bottom of the pan. Fry for about 2 minutes on each side, or until pretty brown (not dark brown, but darker than golden). Remove from the pan and drain on a paper towel to blot the grease. Eat with applesauce or sour cream.

JALAPEÑO CORN POPPERS

This is a quick-and-easy snack that combines spice, cheese and everyone's favorite—the crispiness of fried food! If you want to skip most of the steps and just eat the cheese, I won't hold it against you, but trust me, the extra work will pay off.

MAKES 10 TO 12 POPPERS

2 eggs, beaten

1 cup (125 g) all-purpose flour

1½ tsp (6 g) baking powder

½ tsp salt

¼ cup (43 g) sliced jalapeño pepper

¼ cup (60 ml) milk

1 (12-oz [340-g]) can corn, drained and ¼ cup (60 ml) of the liquid reserved

2 cups (475 ml) canola oil

1 (8-oz [225-g]) block cheddar cheese, cut into ½-x-2½-in (13-mm-x-6-cm) strips

Crack the eggs into a big bowl. Stir in the flour, baking powder, salt, jalapeño, milk, corn and the reserved corn liquid. Use a fork or spoon to mix it up, but not too much; leave it lumpy. Stirring the mix too much will make the poppers rubbery.

Heat the oil in a medium-size frying pan over medium heat. In 3 to 5 minutes test the oil by sprinkling in a little flour. If it sizzles, the oil is hot enough and you're ready. Coat the cheese strips in the batter and use a spoon to place them in the hot oil. It's better to overdo the batter in this step, so the cheese doesn't ooze out and make the oil gross! Let the poppers fry for about 2 minutes on each side, or until brown. Take them out with a slotted spoon and drain on paper towels to blot the oil. They're ready to eat when you can pick them up without flinching.

MAPLE-BACON BROWNIE

This is just another way of borrowing from the bacon-and-chocolate craze, with a little maple flavor thrown into the mix. I love the smell and taste of maple bacon, so I decided to make a brownie with crispy maple bacon inside, topped with maple frosting. It's gooey and crunchy, sweet and salty.

MAKES 1 PORTION, IF YOU'RE IN THE RIGHT STATE OF MIND TO MOW DOWN BROWNIES

8 oz (225 g) thick-cut maple bacon
½ cup (62 g) all-purpose flour
¼ tsp baking powder
⅓ cup (37 g) unsweetened cocoa powder
2 eggs
½ cup (120 ml) vegetable oil
1 cup (200 g) sugar
1 tsp (5 ml) vanilla
¾ cup (180 ml) maple syrup
2 cups (560 g) vanilla frosting

Preheat the oven to 350°F (177°C).

Heat a medium-size frying pan over high heat and cook the bacon for 2 to 3 minutes per side, or until crisp. Drain on paper towels to blot the grease.

Mix together the flour, baking powder and cocoa in a large bowl. In a medium-size bowl beat the eggs with a fork until they're a uniform yellow and add the oil, sugar and vanilla. Mix it all up and stir it into the dry ingredients. Now mix the batter until it's as smooth as you can get it. Cut or crumble the bacon into little pieces and add them to the batter.

Pour the batter into a baking pan. A 9-inch (23-cm) square pan will work, but so will a similar size if you're in a pinch. Bake for 20 minutes. Let cool in the pan for about 10 minutes.

In a stunning twist of crazy-simple, mix the frosting and syrup together in a small bowl until you have a smooth maple colored and flavored frosting. Pour or spread the frosting onto the cooled brownies. The fridge will help the frosting harden.

CHAPTER FOUR

HASSLE-FREE MEALS THAT WILL GET YOU LAID

COOKING TO IMPRESS

Of all the reasons why guys look to other guys for recipes, this is the most common and, I think, the most important. It's no secret that women love being cooked for. And guys who haven't found their comfort level in the kitchen yet need a few handy recipes to lean on in times of need. Take a look, find the dishes that speak to you and your kitchen skill level and tuck the recipes in your back pocket for the next time you've got someone to impress. Don't roll the dice—make something you know will lead to a happy ending!

KICK-ASS FISH TACOS

These are the best fish tacos you will ever have! The fish batter is a little sweet and not too heavy, and the fish comes out juicy and perfectly cooked. But the star of the show is the spicy and sweet coleslaw, which has a much better crunch than lettuce! The toppings are optional, but try it once this way and you'll never go back.

MAKES 2 SERVINGS (2 FISH TACOS)

SLAW

½ ripe mango
⅛ habanero pepper
1 cup (85 g) coleslaw mix (veggies only!)
Pinch of salt
Pinch of sugar
¼ cup (55 ml) mayo

TARTAR SAUCE

½ dill pickle
¼ cup (55 g) mayo

FOR THE FISH

5 oz (140 g) haddock
2 cups (475 ml) canola oil
1 cup (125 g) all-purpose flour
1 tsp (4 g) baking powder
Pinch of salt
1 cup (240 ml) favorite beer

TO SERVE

2 (6-inch [15-cm]) flour tortillas
1 ripe avocado
1 vine-ripe tomato
2 tbsp (30 ml) sour cream

MAKING THE SLAW

Try to locate the pit in the mango. Cut the flesh off in chunks, with the skin on, avoiding the pit. Once you have the mango in pieces, use a spoon to separate the flesh from the skin. Or, save yourself a lot of trouble and buy already peeled and cut mango at the grocery store. Chop the mango flesh into small pieces. Cut the habanero pepper into fine pieces, trying not to include any seeds. Transfer the mango and pepper to a small bowl and add the slaw mix, salt, sugar and mayo. Set aside.

MAKING THE TARTAR SAUCE

Cut the pickle into tiny pieces. In a small bowl mix them with the mayo.

COOKING THE FISH

Cut the fish into 6 equal chunks. Heat the oil in a medium-size frying pan over medium heat. Meanwhile, in a small bowl, mix the flour, baking powder, salt and beer. Mix the batter until it is smooth, without any lumps. Test to see if the oil is hot enough by dropping a little batter into it. If it sizzles right away, the oil is hot enough.

Put the chunks of fish into the batter, coating them completely. Place them in the oil, one at a time, moving them after about 30 seconds so they don't stick to the bottom of the pan. Cook the fish for about 3 to 4 minutes, or until golden and cooked through, turning the pieces after about 2 minutes. With a slotted spoon, transfer to paper towels to drain.

SERVE IT UP

Microwave the tortillas for 15 seconds. Place each one on a plate and smear the tartar sauce evenly on both tortillas. Cut the avocado into 8 slices and put 4 on each taco. Dice the tomato and put a few spoonfuls on each taco. Put 3 pieces of fish onto each taco. Finally, heap the slaw on top. Bang, that's two fish tacos!

STUFFED STEAK WITH CREAMY MUSHROOM RIGATONI

The only thing better than slow-cooked steak is slow-cooked steak stuffed with cheese and eaten over pasta. This traditional Italian dish—the stuffed steak is called a braciola—is easier than it sounds and is as impressive as hell.

MAKES 2 SERVINGS

1 (10-oz [280-g]) flank steak

2 tbsp (30 g) unsalted butter

½ white onion, sliced into strips

2 cloves garlic

2 slices day-old bread, cut into ½-in (13-mm) chunks

1 tbsp (3 g) dried basil

2 tsp (10 g) salt

2 razor-thin slices prosciutto

½ cup (56 g) shredded mozzarella

2 tbsp (30 ml) olive oil

2 cups (475 ml) traditional tomato sauce

1 cup (116 g) rigatoni

½ cup (30 g) sliced medium-size mushrooms

1 cup (254 g) cannellini beans, rinsed and drained

1 tsp (2 g) red pepper flakes

Lay the flank steak down on a cutting board. Use a meat tenderizer (meat hammer), rolling pin or a mug to carefully pound the steak flat. Once your steak is almost see-through, find the lines that run across the steak, which are called the "grain." You will want to arrange your filling so that you can roll the steak up with the grain running across the whole length of the roll. When you cut the stuffed steak, you'll be cutting across the grain, which will make the meat easier to chew.

To make the stuffing, melt the butter in a cast-iron skillet over medium-high heat, add the onions, and cook for 2 or 3 minutes or until it begins to soften. Crush the garlic with a fork, cut it into small pieces and toss them into the pan. Add the bread and cook, stirring with a wooden spoon so the bread absorbs as much of the garlic butter as possible. Add the basil and 1 teaspoon (5 g) of the salt and mix it up. Cook until all of the ingredients are soft, about 5 minutes altogether. Set aside.

Preheat the oven to 400°F (204°C).

To stuff the steak, lay the prosciutto slices over the steak so that the grain of prosciutto runs in the same direction as the grain of the steak. Next add half of the cheese and then all of the bread stuffing, making a mound that runs the length of your steak, like a burrito. Top the stuffing with the remaining cheese. Now roll the steak up, like a wrap or a burrito.

Heat 1 tablespoon (15 ml) of the olive oil in the skillet over medium-high heat. Put the steak roll in the skillet and brown for 1 minute on each side. Pour the tomato sauce into the skillet and over the steak. Put the skillet into the oven and cook the meat, uncovered, for 40 minutes. Lower the heat to 350°F (177°C) and cook for 25 more minutes.

When you've lowered the heat in the oven, fill a medium-size pot with water and bring to a boil. Cook the rigatoni according to the package directions until tender. Drain well in a colander. Meanwhile, heat the remaining 1 tablespoon (15 ml) of olive oil in the pot over medium heat. Add the mushrooms and cook for 3 to 4 minutes, or until they soften, moving them around with a wooden spoon. Add the beans and cooked pasta. Mix it up and season it with the remaining 1 teaspoon (5 g) of salt and the red pepper flakes.

Remove the meat from the pan and cut crosswise into 1-inch-(2.5-cm-) thick medallions. Divide the pasta between 2 plates and place the meat on top. Spoon the tomato sauce over all.

BONE-IN RIB EYE WITH SAUTÉED SPINACH AND FETA

Rib eye is my favorite cut of steak. I love the fat content and I really enjoy panfrying them. This recipe uses the natural flavors of feta cheese and roasted garlic to flavor a great steak and make a nice sauce to eat it with. It's also a one-pan dish, so very little cleanup is necessary.

MAKES 2 SERVINGS

1 tsp (15 ml) olive oil
2 (10-oz [280-g]) bone-in rib eye steaks
Black pepper to taste
¼ cup (40 g) roasted garlic cloves
½ cup (55 g) crumbled feta cheese
2 cups (60 g) fresh baby spinach
1–2 tbsp (15–30 ml) water, as needed
Pinch of salt (optional)

Heat the oil in a large frying pan over medium heat. Meanwhile, season the rib eye with black pepper. The feta is very salty, so don't add salt until you're done; you may not need it. Put the steaks into the hot oil and cook for about 2 minutes per side, or until browned. Take them out of the pan, leaving the juices behind.

Add the garlic and feta cheese to the same pan, still over medium heat, and cook, using a wooden spoon to break the feta apart and work it into the juices from the steak. Add the spinach and stir it into the liquid in the pan. If the liquid is evaporating too fast add 1 to 2 tablespoons (15–30 ml) of water. Put your steaks back into the pan and cover. Let them cook 5 to 10 minutes, depending on how well done you like your steaks.

Put the steaks on plates and pour the spinach, feta and garlic sauce over them. Taste and sprinkle with salt if needed.

EGGPLANT ROLL UPS

This recipe was re-created from a dish I ate at a wedding I went to last summer. Every once in a while something is so good that you just have to find out how they did it, and this one is surprisingly easy. The chef told me that his secret to the crêpe-like texture of the eggplant was the egg wash, and I find that it works great. Feel free to fill the eggplant with anything you want—it's just a canvas for you to paint!

MAKES 2 SERVINGS (6 ROLL UPS)

1 eggplant, skin on

2 eggs

2 tbsp (23 g) grated Parmesan cheese

2 tbsp (30 ml) olive oil

1 cup (230 g) ricotta cheese

2 tsp (10 g) salt

Pinch of black pepper

2 tsp (6 g) granulated garlic

6 razor-thin slices prosciutto

1 vine-ripe tomato

½ cup (56 g) shredded mozzarella

Preheat the oven to 425°F (218°C).

Cut the eggplant lengthwise into ¼-inch-(6-mm-) thick slices. If that's too tough, just cut them as thin as you can. Crack the eggs into a shallow bowl and stir in the Parmesan cheese. Heat 1 tablespoon (15 ml) of the olive oil in a large frying pan over medium-high heat. Dip one eggplant slice into the egg and put it in the frying pan. Cook for 1 to 2 minutes per side, or until light brown. Drain on paper towels to blot the oil. Repeat with the remaining eggplant slices.

In a small bowl mix the ricotta, 1 teaspoon (5 g) of the salt, black pepper and 1 teaspoon (3 g) of the garlic. Use a fork to mix until smooth.

Lay out an eggplant slice and put a slice of prosciutto on top. Next spoon some of the ricotta mix over the prosciutto and roll it up like a little burrito. Put it into a cast-iron skillet or a baking pan, seam-side down. Repeat until all the rollups are in the pan.

Cut your tomato into thin slices (wash it first!) and toss them with the remaining 1 tablespoon (15 ml) of olive oil, 1 teaspoon (5 g) of salt and 1 teaspoon (3 g) of garlic. Put the tomato slices on top of the eggplant roll ups, and sprinkle the mozzarella over the top. Put the pan into the oven and bake for 20 to 25 minutes, or until the cheese browns.

ROAST LAMB WITH PINEAPPLE AND CREAMY RISOTTO

This recipe has one of the most impressive flavor combinations in this book. It is guaranteed to live up to its chapter title! Warm pineapple (a natural aphrodisiac, by the way) complements the slightly gamey and naturally fatty nature of the lamb. The colors add even more to the wow factor. Best part? This will be the least laborsome part of your night!

MAKES 2 SERVINGS

1 whole pineapple
Pinch of salt

RISOTTO

2 tbsp plus 1½ tsp (40 ml) olive oil
1 small white onion, chopped
1 clove garlic, chopped
1 cup (220 g) Arborio rice
1 tbsp (7 g) ground coriander
1 tsp (5 g) salt
1 tsp (2 g) black pepper
3 cups (700 ml) chicken stock

1½ tsp (8 ml) olive oil
4 small lamb shanks (about 8 oz [230 g] total)
Pinch of salt
Pinch of pepper
½ cup (115 g) ricotta cheese
1 tbsp (20 ml) apricot marmalade
Pinch of cayenne pepper
1 tbsp (22 ml) pomegranate molasses

Preheat the oven to 450°F (232°C).

Cut the ends off the pineapple first, then the sides, and finally the remaining corners. Cut the pineapple lengthwise into rectangular pieces about the size of a 3-x-5-in (7.6-x-13-cm) index card. Lightly salt the pineapple, place the slices on a baking sheet and roast in the oven for 15 minutes, or until browned and very soft. Cut the pineapple crosswise into ¼-inch (6-mm) strips and set aside.

While the pineapple is roasting, heat 1½ teaspoons (8 ml) of the olive oil in a deep frying pan over high heat. Add the onion and garlic and cook, stirring occasionally with a wooden spoon, for 3 minutes. Add the remaining oil and stir in the rice, coriander, salt and pepper and cook, stirring, for 2 to 3 minutes to lightly brown the rice. Add 1 cup (240 ml) of the stock, stirring constantly to prevent the rice from burning. When most of the liquid is absorbed, add another 1 cup (240 ml) of stock, and when most of it has been absorbed add the remaining 1 cup (240 ml) cup of stock. When that is also mostly absorbed, reduce the heat to low and cover the rice, and cook, stirring occasionally.

To cook the lamb shanks, heat the olive oil in a large frying pan over medium heat. Season the lamb shanks lightly with salt and pepper. Cook, uncovered, for 4 to 5 minutes, without stirring, until browned on the bottom. Flip to the other side, cover the pan and cook for another 3 to 5 minutes, or until browned.

In the meantime put the ricotta cheese in a mixing bowl and whisk in the apricot marmalade and cayenne pepper.

When everything is ready, divide the risotto between 2 plates and scatter 1 teaspoon (5 g) dollops of the ricotta onto the risotto. Place 2 lamb shanks in the center of the risotto on each plate, and 3 to 4 pineapple strips on and around the lamb. Drizzle the molasses over all and serve.

LAMB PILAF

Lamb pilaf is a dish we started serving on our food truck this past season, and it quickly became our customers' favorite side! Lamb is such a buttery flavor; it adds a creaminess to the pilaf that goes well with fresh veggies.

MAKES 3 SERVINGS AS A SIDE DISH

1 tsp (5 ml) olive oil

1 clove garlic, minced

½ white onion, chopped

1 carrot, peeled and chopped

¼ cup (43 g) orzo

1 cup (240 ml) lamb juice from cooking
(p. 114 or 123)

1 cup (240 ml) water

Pinch of salt

Pinch of ground cumin

1 cup (210 g) jasmine rice

Heat the olive oil in a large frying pan over medium-high heat. Add the garlic, onions, carrot and orzo and cook, keeping them moving with a wooden spoon so they don't burn. After about 3 minutes, or when the onion and garlic are lightly browned, add the lamb juice, water, salt and cumin. Bring to a simmer, so the liquid is bubbling lightly.

Add the rice and stir it in so everything is well mixed. Turn the heat down to low and cover the pan. Cook the pilaf for 25 to 30 minutes, or until the liquid in the pan has evaporated and the rice is soft enough to eat. Keep your eye on the pan and turn the heat down if needed to keep the liquid from evaporating too quickly, which will burn the rice. You're all set!

FRESH TUNA SALAD WITH GOAT CHEESE AND GINGER WALNUTS

This is the perfect recipe for impressing a girl. It's light and won't have her worried that you're trying to fatten her up, but it's complex enough that she'll think you spent all day preparing it. The two trickiest parts are cooking the tuna and candying the walnuts. My advice, if you've got a hot date: Do the nuts in advance so they're ready. The tuna? Use an instant-read thermometer to check whether it's done and you'll be covered. Good luck!

MAKES 2 SERVINGS

¼ cup (60 ml) soy sauce

¼ cup (60 ml) rice wine vinegar

1 (8-oz [230-g]) tuna fillet, about ½-inch (13-mm) thick

4 tbsp (60 g) unsalted butter

1 (1-in [2.5-cm]) piece fresh ginger

1 tbsp (13 g) brown sugar

¼ cup (30 g) shelled walnut halves

2 tbsp (30 ml) olive oil

½ cup (80 g) sesame seeds

1 head Boston or Bibb Lettuce

½ cup (80 g) grape tomatoes, halved

4 oz (115 g) fresh goat cheese

2 tbsp (30 ml) balsamic vinegar

1 tbsp (21 ml) honey

¼ cup (30 g) wasabi peas (optional)

In a zipper-top bag, mix the soy sauce and rice wine vinegar. Cut the tuna into 4 equal pieces and put them into the bag. Seal the bag and refrigerate for at least 30 minutes and up to 12 hours.

To candy the nuts, melt the butter in a medium-size frying pan over medium heat. Use a cheese grater to shave the ginger into the pan, and stir in the brown sugar. Add the walnuts and cook for about 4–5 minutes, stirring the walnuts constantly, until they are completely coated with the butter and sugar mix and the mix has thickened. Remove the pan from the heat and place the nuts on a plate lined with wax paper. Throw it in the fridge to cool.

When you're ready to cook the tuna, remove it from the marinade and pat dry with a paper towel. Heat the olive oil in a large frying pan over medium-high heat. Put the sesame seeds in a shallow dish, and roll the tuna in the sesame seeds so that all sides of each piece are completely covered. Sear the tuna in the pan on each side evenly for about 4–5 minutes per side, or until the sesame seeds are golden brown. If you have an instant-read thermometer, it should register 135°F (57°C).

Line 2 dinner plates with the lettuce and scatter the grape tomato halves on top. Scatter 4 or 5 pieces of the goat cheese over each plate, followed by a handful of the coated nuts. Splash the balsamic vinegar over the greens. Place 2 pieces of tuna in the center of each salad and drizzle the honey over the top.

Add the wasabi peas last, if you're up for a little bit of crunch and some serious kick!

RASPBERRY-APRICOT SALAD

This salad is proof that you don't have to complicate food to make it great. I make this salad for most family holiday gatherings, and everyone always raves about it. Add a cold piece of grilled chicken, and you've got a great lunch or even a simple dinner.

MAKES 2 LARGE SALADS

DRESSING

1 lemon
2 tbsp (40 ml) raspberry preserves
¼ cup (60 ml) extra-virgin olive oil
Salt and black pepper to taste

2 cups (40 g) arugula
1 cup (30 g) baby spinach
¼ cup (38 g) dried apricots, sliced
1 tbsp (6 g) sliced almonds

With a lemon zester, vegetable peeler or small paring knife, remove a few pieces of the yellow skin, or zest, of the lemon (but none of the white under layer, which is super bitter and will ruin the flavor). Put into a small bowl. Cut the lemon in half and squeeze all of the juice into the bowl. With a fork, stir in the raspberry preserves and slowly beat in the olive oil. You may not need all of the oil; stop when the dressing has the right consistency. Season with salt and pepper.

Put the arugula and spinach in a salad bowl. Drizzle the dressing lightly over the greens and mix. Add the apricots and almonds, toss it all together and serve.

DEEP-FRIED SWEET POTATO SALAD

Making a salad is like playing the guitar—almost anyone can do it, but very few people can do it really well. A friend of mine introduced me to the idea of crispy sweet potatoes as a salad topping and those, along with really fresh veggies and this honey dressing, make for a sweet and crunchy salad.

MAKES 1 SERVING

½ cup (120 ml) water

2 tsp (10 g) sugar

¼ cup (28 g) cashews

¼ cup (60 ml) extra-virgin olive oil

¼ cup (60 ml) fresh lemon juice

1 tsp (7 ml) honey

2 cups (475 ml) canola oil

½ cup (90 g) thin strips sweet potato

2 cups (40 g) mixed salad greens

¼ cup (40 g) grape tomatoes, halved

5 slices English cucumber (the long seedless kind)

Pinch of salt

Pinch of cracked black pepper

To candy the cashews, combine the water, sugar and cashews in a small saucepan over medium-high heat. Boil for 2 minutes, stirring to prevent the nuts from burning. Remove the nuts with a slotted spoon and put them on a plate lined with wax paper to cool and harden.

To make the dressing, combine the olive oil, lemon juice and honey in a small saucepan over medium-low heat. Cook, stirring, until the honey dissolves into the oil and lemon juice. Remove from the heat.

Heat the canola oil in a medium-size frying pan over medium-high heat for about 3 minutes. Add the sweet potato strips and fry until crispy and light brown, which should take 2 minutes, depending on how thin you got them. Remove with a slotted spoon and drain on paper towels.

In a medium bowl, combine the greens, tomatoes, cucumber, candied cashews, salt, pepper and salad dressing. Mix the salad really well so all the good stuff will be in every bite. Heap on a plate and put the fried sweet potatoes on top. Enjoy!

CHEESY POTATO SOUP

This is one of my favorite recipes for a few reasons: The first is that I love how awesome cheese tastes in soup. But more importantly, this soup can be used so many different ways. It's heavy enough to be a meal, and it's super quick and easy—if your potatoes were already cooked or you used a microwave to soften them, you could make this soup in 10 minutes! Finally, this soup is really cheap to make. Sub in pre-grated Parm, and this soup could be made for less than a few bucks per person. Get to it!

MAKES 2 SERVINGS

HERBED BREAD (OPTIONAL)
Olive oil or melted butter for brushing the bread

1 loaf Italian or French bread

¼ cup (7 g) Italian seasoning or dried basil

1 tbsp (6 g) red pepper flakes

1 leek, washed well

1 shallot

1 clove garlic

½ cup (120 g) unsalted butter

2 medium-size white potatoes

½ cup (62 g) all-purpose flour

8 cups (2 L) water, plus extra for covering the potatoes

2 tbsp (30 g) salt

1 tbsp (6 g) black pepper

1 cup (180 g) grated Parmesan cheese

¼ cup (10 g) finely chopped fresh flat-leaf parsley

Got some bread? Preheat the oven to 375°F (191°C). Brush a thin layer of olive oil or butter over the bread and sprinkle with some Italian seasoning or dried basil and the red pepper flakes. Warm in the oven for a few minutes, until the crust is toasted. Serve whole or cut into ½-inch-(13-mm-) thick slices. Set aside and make the soup.

Cut off the dark green part the leek and toss it. Cut the light green and white parts into ⅛-inch-(3-mm-) thick rings. Peel and finely chop the shallot. Crush the garlic with a fork and mince.

Melt the butter a medium-size frying pan over high heat and add the leek, shallot and garlic. Cook, stirring occasionally, for about 5 minutes, or until soft. Set aside.

Wash and peel the potatoes and cut into ¼-inch (6-m) dice. Transfer to a small bowl, cover with water and set aside.

Transfer the veggies and butter in the frying pan to a medium-size to large soup pot and set it over medium-high heat. Whisk in the flour, 1 tablespoon (8 g) at a time. When the mixture becomes pastelike, whisk in the water, 1 cup (240 ml) at a time, making sure to eliminate any lumps. Raise the heat up to high, add the salt, black pepper and the potatoes and cook, covered, for 10 minutes or until the potatoes are tender.

Set aside a small handful of the cheese. Whisk the rest into the soup gradually, making sure it melts into the soup. Ladle the soup into bowls. Garnish with the chopped parsley and a light sprinkle of the remaining cheese.

SLOW-COOKED LAMB AND EASY BEET TURNIP PUREE

Braising meat gives it a tasty outside and will keep the meat juicy inside. This recipe will give you a really tender piece of lamb and the beets and turnips you cook with the lamb will turn into a delicious starch on the side. Turnip for what?

MAKES 2 SERVINGS

2 tbsp (30 ml) olive oil

1 (3-lb [1.3-kg]) boneless leg of lamb

2 tsp (10 g) salt

2 tsp (4 g) cracked pepper

1 tsp (2 g) ground cinnamon

1 tsp (4 g) granulated sugar

2 carrots, diced but not peeled

1 beet, peeled and diced

1 cup (240 ml) sweet white wine

2 turnips, peeled and diced

½ cup (120 g) unsalted butter, melted

2 tbsp (26 g) brown sugar

4 fresh parsley sprigs (optional)

Preheat the oven to 225°F (107°C).

Heat the olive oil in a large frying pan over high heat, or on a griddle top, which is really cool to have. Season the lamb with the salt, pepper, cinnamon and granulated sugar. Brown the lamb in the oil for about 2 to 3 minutes on each side until browned evenly all over. Transfer the lamb and its juices to an ovenproof pan and add the carrots, beet, wine and turnips. Seal the pan tightly with foil and put it into the oven for 6 to 8 hours. I like to braise for as long as possible, but after 6 hours, you should be in good shape.

Take the beet and turnips out of the pan (but not the carrots) and put them in a food processor or blender. Add the butter and brown sugar, as well as ½ cup (120 ml) of the juices from the pan. Blend until smooth.

Divide the puree between 2 plates, set the lamb and carrots on top. If you're feeling fancy, add some parsley for a garnish.

STUFFED CORNISH HENS

Cornish hens are as easy to cook as chickens, but for some reason there's a personal pan pizza aspect to them that makes people think they're fancy. Go with them, stuff them with this very cool bagel stuffing, and enjoy the evening.

MAKES 2 SERVINGS

2 Cornish game hens

2 bagels from a bakery (1 or 2 days old is best)

½ cup (120 g) unsalted butter

½ onion, chopped fine

2 cloves garlic, minced

1 stalk celery, chopped fine

2 cups (475 ml) chicken broth

1 tsp (1 g) dried basil

1 tsp (5 g) salt

Black pepper to taste

1–2 tbsp (8–16 g) all-purpose flour

Preheat the oven to 400°F (204°C).

Rinse the hens with cold water inside and out. Pat dry with paper towels.

Cut the bagels into bite-size pieces. Melt the butter in a medium-size saucepan or pot over medium heat. Stir in the onion, garlic and celery and cook, stirring occasionally, for 4 to 5 minutes, or until you can almost see through the onion. Stir in 1 cup (240 ml) of the chicken broth, basil, and salt and season with pepper. Bring up to a boil, remove from the heat and immediately stir in the bagel pieces.

Carefully spoon the stuffing into the hens, putting in as much as you can fit. Put the hens in a baking pan or roasting pan and roast for 45 minutes or until they register 165°F (74°C) on an instant-read thermometer inserted into the thickest part of the breast. (Being too cool for a thermometer means you'll have to cut into the chicken to make sure it's cooked through, in which case, the results of this meal are no longer guaranteed—ha ha.)

Remove the hens from the oven and place on serving plates to rest. Drain the pan drippings into a small saucepan and heat over medium heat. Add 1 to 2 tablespoons (8 to 16 g) of the flour and cook for 2 minutes, stirring constantly, to make a smooth paste. Slowly add the remaining 1 cup (240 ml) of chicken broth, stirring until smooth. Cut each hen in half on a cutting board.

Serve the hens, stuffing-side up, smothered in gravy.

BEEF MEDIUM-WELLINGTON

Beef Wellington is a classic high-end dish that will impress your date immediately. The theatrics alone of cutting open the perfectly browned puff pastry and releasing the juices from the beautifully prepared filet are worth the effort of making this recipe. And the flavorful steak, bacon and blue cheese combo is perfect with the spicy ketchup!

MAKES 2 SUPER-SEXY SERVINGS

2 strips bacon, chopped fine

1 cup (230 g) unsalted butter

½ cup (30 g) mushrooms

1 (1-lb [455-g]) filet mignon

Pinch of salt

Pinch of black pepper

¼ cup (34 g) blue cheese

1 (10-inch [25-cm]) square puff pastry sheet, thawed

2 eggs, lightly beaten

2 tbsp (34 ml) ketchup

2 tsp (10 ml) sriracha sauce

Preheat your oven to 350°F (177°C)

Put the bacon in a large frying pan over medium-high heat and let it sit for 1 minute, or until it begins to sizzle. Cook, keep it moving with a wooden spoon, and add the butter and mushrooms. Season the steak with salt and pepper and add the steak to the pan, clearing enough space with your spoon for the steak to touch the bottom of the frying pan so that it browns. It should take 1 minute on each side for the steak to brown, leaving it underdone enough so when it bakes it won't overcook. Once the steak is browned on both sides, remove the pan from the heat and take the steak out of the pan. Stir the blue cheese into the mix in the pan.

On a baking sheet coated with nonstick cooking spray, unfold the puff pastry sheet so it's flat. Sit the steak in the middle and carefully spoon the mushroom, bacon and blue cheese mix over it, so the whole top is covered. Fold the puff pastry sheet around the steak so that the steak is enclosed and pinch the edges of the puff pastry together so that they stick. Brush the top with the beaten egg using a paper towel.

Put the beef in the oven and bake for about 25 to 30 minutes, or until the pastry puffs up and browns on top. Remove it from the oven and let the steak rest on the pan for 5 minutes so the juices are sealed in.

Mix the ketchup and sriracha together—simple and easy, but tangy and perfect for this dish!

Transfer the beef to a serving plate, and cut it in half at the table. Eat this with a steak knife and a fork, slicing across so every bite has pastry, steak and cheesy bacon goodness!

HELP YOURSELF TO SECONDS

CHAPTER FIVE

REPURPOSING YOUR LEFTOVERS

The toughest part of cooking for one is trying to make batches that only one person is going to eat. It's OK to make a little extra; I found a few cool things to do with all those leftovers. Turn your leftover buffalo chicken dip into mouth-watering heuvos rancheros. Got some extra mashed potatoes? How 'bout some pasta? The best part about these recipes for leftovers is that it doesn't really matter exactly what you've got left; they're designed to transform almost anything into an interesting and fresh new dish. Some of them are so good, you'll be cooking extra just to try them out!

HASHING IT OUT IN THE MORNING

Even better than a good wake-and-bake dish is a no-bake hash that is made with leftover meat and only a few other ingredients. I used brisket for mine, but really any meat or chicken will work. For the vegetarians? Try the home fries.

MAKES 2 LARGE SERVINGS

8 oz (230 g) leftover cooked brisket

1 white onion, chopped

1 potato, skin on

2 cloves garlic

1–4 tbsp (15–60 ml) olive oil

1 tsp (5 g) salt

½ tsp black pepper

4 oz (115 g) of your favorite shredded cheese

Using a meat grinder or a sharp knife (because let's face it, who has a meat grinder?), chop up the meat, onion, and potato into small pieces, ¼ inch (6 mm) or less (larger than that and potato and onion might not cook). Mix it all together in medium-size bowl. Crush the garlic with a fork, mince and add to the bowl.

Heat 1 tablespoon (15 ml) of the olive oil in a large frying pan over high heat. Add the hash to the pan so that it covers the bottom in a thin layer, no more than ½ inch (13 mm). If your pan isn't big enough, fry in batches and add more oil between batches as needed. Brown the hash, stirring every minute or so at first to make sure that it browns well and adding pinches of the salt and pepper a couple of times as you cook. When each batch of hash is close to being well browned, in about 10 minutes, reduce the heat to low and stir in the shredded cheese. Remove from the heat as soon as the cheese is melted and bubbly and grab a couple of plates and forks.

REASON-FOR-HOSTING BREAD PUDDING

Anyone who has ever hosted a big family gathering on a holiday or a get-together with friends knows that it's a pain in the ass cleaning up the place and feeding a bunch of hungry people. The payoff? If your friends have any class, they leave behind all the leftover desserts and booze. I like to leave the kitchen mess for morning cleanup and reward myself by baking off a heart-stopping dessert mash-up while I wash dishes and wipe counters. The gooey sweetness from this leftover bread pudding will be motivation enough to host your friends' next get-together! And if you have any leftovers from this mashup, slice it up, soak it in egg, and make French toast with it. French toast from cheesecake and apple pie? Yup, it's that good.

MAKES 2 LARGE SERVINGS

½ cup leftover cheesecake

½ cup leftover coffee cake

½ cup leftover apple pie

½ cup leftover chocolate chip cookies

2 cups (170 g) diced leftover Portuguese sweet bread (medium dice)

4 eggs

¼ cup (60 ml) cream

Preheat the oven to 350°F (177°C).

Break up the cakes, pie and cookies into pieces about the same size as the sweet bread so the pudding won't be lumpy. In a large mixing bowl, mix the leftover desserts with the bread. In a medium-size bowl, beat the eggs and cream together with a fork to blend well. Pour into the bowl with the desserts and mix it up fairly well, letting the bread absorb the egg.

Pour the mixture into a baking pan or a cast-iron skillet, filling the entire pan. Place the pan in the oven and bake for about 25 minutes, or until the top is firm in the middle and a knife inserted in the pudding comes out dry. Let it cool and eat one chunk at a time.

BUFFALO CHICKEN HUEVOS RANCHEROS

This huevos rancheros recipe makes great use of the leftover Buffalo Chicken Queso (p. 79) you and your buddies didn't finish. It's not as traditional as the classic version I usually make, but it's really easy to make and has every bit as much flavor.

MAKES 1 SERVING

2 eggs

1 tsp (5 ml) milk

1 tsp (5 g) unsalted butter

½ cup (70 g) leftover Buffalo Chicken Queso (p. 79)

2 (6-in [15-cm]) flour tortillas

1 avocado

In a small bowl, beat the eggs and milk with a fork until smooth.

Melt the butter in a small frying pan over medium heat and add the eggs. Scramble the eggs, using a plastic spatula to scrape them repeatedly from the sides and bottom of the pan as the eggs cook. In about 2 minutes they should be fully cooked.

Put the queso leftovers in a microwave-safe bowl and nuke for 30 seconds on high power.

Lay the tortillas flat on a plate. Cut the avocado lengthwise into 8 slices, and divide them between the 2 tortillas. Divide the eggs evenly between them and put them on top of the avocado. Top it all by pouring your queso over the eggs. Dig in!

LEFTOVER POTATO GNOCCHI

This pasta dish seems crazy-complicated, but it's actually really easy and can be made with the leftover mashed potatoes sitting in your fridge. With just a few other ingredients and in a short period of time, you can have homemade gnocchi. If you're in a rush, skip the creamy sauce and go for the canned stuff!

MAKES 1 LARGE SERVING

GNOCCHI

1 egg
½ cup (105 g) leftover mashed potatoes
½ cup (62 g) all-purpose flour
½ cup (120 ml) water
2 pinches salt
Pinch of black pepper

SAUCE

1 tbsp (15 g) unsalted butter
1 clove garlic
½ cup (120 ml) cream
1 tsp (3 g) cornstarch
¼ cup (60 ml) water
Pinch of salt

MAKING THE GNOCCHI

Fill a medium-size pot with water and bring to a boil over high heat. Crack the egg into a large bowl and beat it with a fork until it's smooth. Add the mashed potatoes, flour, ½ cup (120 ml) water, salt and pepper and mix them until they start to form a dough. With clean hands, start kneading the dough, or working it with your hands to form a ball, squeezing it flat and rerolling it until the dough is smooth. On a cutting board or clean countertop, roll the dough into little logs about 1-inch (2.5 cm) long and ½-inch (13 mm) wide. Roll the gnocchi along the tines of a fork to flatten them just a little bit, leaving light indentations in the dough. Put the gnocchi into the boiling water for 15 to 20 minutes, or until they float to the top and are very tender to the touch. Drain well.

MAKING THE SAUCE

While the gnocchi cook, melt the butter in a small saucepan over medium heat. Crush the garlic with a fork and add it to the butter. Mix it with a wooden spoon, add the cream and let it bubble in the pan for 3 or 4 minutes. Stir the cornstarch into the water in a small bowl and add the water to the cream. (Don't skip the separate bowl step, or the cornstarch won't thicken the sauce!) Turn down the heat to low and cook, stirring for 5 minutes, or until the sauce has thickened. Add the salt and remove from the heat.

Pour the sauce over the gnocchi and eat.

FRIED LASAGNA

Fried mac and cheese balls are a classic and one of my favorites. I stumbled on this recipe when I found myself with some leftover lasagna and a little time to kill. The biggest difference between using lasagna and mac and cheese is that the lasagna needs more help holding together. Make sure to cut the lasagna up and mix it well with the cornmeal, so it doesn't fall apart when it fries.

MAKES 2 SERVINGS (4 TO 6 FRIED LASAGNA BALLS)

1 cup leftover lasagna (p. 58), chopped up
1 cup (120 g) cornmeal
2 eggs
¼ cup (45 g) grated Parmesan cheese
2 cups (475 ml) canola oil

Cut up the lasagna into small chunks. In a medium-size bowl, mix the lasagna with ¼ cup (30 g) of the cornmeal. With clean hands shape the lasagna into 2-inch (5-cm) balls.

Crack the eggs into a shallow bowl and beat lightly with a fork. In another shallow bowl, mix the remaining ¾ cup (90 g) of the cornmeal with the Parm. Dip the balls into the egg and then roll them in the cornmeal mix and set aside.

Heat the oil in a small saucepan over medium-high. It will take a few minutes for the oil to get hot; check it with a few sprinkles of cornmeal. If they sizzle right away, the oil is ready. Fry the balls, a few at a time, until golden brown, turning them to brown all over. Remove them from the oil with a slotted spoon and drain on paper towels.

POT ROAST STEAK BOMB

Sometimes the simplest and most obvious recipes are the best. No doubt this is a sandwich you could figure out on your own, but I figured I'd give you a head start using leftover pot roast. The key for me is melting and mixing the cheese into the juices from the roast. In the end there is a saucy quality about the cheese that makes it a perfect leftover sammy.

MAKES 1 FAT SAMMY

1 tbsp (15 ml) olive oil

5 oz (140 g) leftover pot roast (p. 24)

½ white onion, sliced thin

1 green or red bell pepper, sliced thin

1 bakery-fresh French roll

1 tbsp (14 ml) mayo

3 slices of your favorite cheese

Heat the oil in a large frying pan over medium heat. Cut the pot roast into thin slices if you can. If not, small chunks will work. Put the meat into the pan, leave it for 1 minute and then cook, stirring, until the meat has started browning. Add the onion and pepper and cook, stirring once every minute or so to keep the meat and veggies from burning, until the veggies are tender and meat is browned.

Cut the French roll open and spread the mayo on the roll. Add the cheese to the almost-ready meat and give it 30 seconds to begin melting. Stir carefully, and tuck the cheesy steak and veggies into the roll. It's ready.

MASHED POTATO PIE

Meals made from leftovers should be easy to make, and this recipe fits the bill; it's basically a pot pie with no crust to make or bake. I used chopped chicken but any leftover meat would work.

MAKES 1 SERVING

2 tbsp (30 ml) olive oil
½ cup (62 g) canned corn, drained
1 carrot, peeled and chopped
2 cups (421 g) leftover mashed potatoes
2 tsp (2 g) black pepper
1 tsp (5 g) salt
½ cup (120 ml) gravy
1 cup (125 g) chopped leftover cooked chicken

Preheat the oven to 400°F (204°C).

Heat 1 tablespoon (15 ml) of the olive oil in a medium-size frying pan over medium heat. Add the corn and carrots and cook for 5 minutes, stirring occasionally. Set aside.

Spread half of the mashed potatoes across the bottom and up the sides of a large cast-iron skillet. In a small bowl, mix together the rest of the potatoes with the remaining 1 tablespoon (15 ml) of the olive oil, the black pepper and salt.

Pour the gravy into the potato shell and add the chicken, corn and carrot. Spread out the potato and olive oil mix on top and place the pie in the oven. Bake for 35 minutes, or until the potatoes have browned on top.

CHILI-CHEESE-FRY FRITTATA

The easiest thing I can think to do the morning after making a pot of chili is mix it up with some eggs. A frittata is basically a baked omelet, and it's a lot easier and requires less attention to get right. Just bake it up and enjoy the chili all over again.

MAKES 2 SERVINGS

4 eggs
¼ cup (60 ml) milk
1 cup (180 g) peeled and cubed potato
1 cup (160 g) leftover chili (p. 64)
½ cup (60 g) shredded cheddar cheese
Salt and black pepper to taste

Preheat the oven to 350°F (177°C).

Beat the eggs with a fork in a large bowl until they are a uniform yellow. Add the milk and mix well. Stir in the potatoes, chili and cheese.

Pour the mix into a cast-iron skillet or another ovenproof pan. Season with salt and pepper. Bake for 35 to 40 minutes, or until the eggs are firm in the center and the tip of a knife inserted in the frittata comes out dry.

SPINACH PESTO RAVIOLI WITH MEAT GRAVY

Ravioli are a great way to use your leftovers and make a brand-new meal out of them. Pasta isn't easy to make, but once you get a feel for it, you'll end up stuffing ravioli with almost anything. This recipe would work well with leftovers from a steak or pot roast and salad. Use your spinach to make a quick pesto filling, and always save the juice from cooking meat to make a great gravy down the road.

SERVES 1–2 (MAKES 10–12 RAVIOLI)

1½ cups (185 g) all-purpose flour

2 eggs

1 tsp (3 g) granulated garlic

1 tsp (15 g) salt

1 tsp (2 g) black pepper

1 cup (30 g) fresh spinach

½ cup (90 g) grated Parmesan cheese

½ cup (120 ml) olive oil, or as needed

1 cup (240 ml) leftover meat stock

1 tsp (3 g) cornstarch

½ cup (120 ml) water

1 tsp (15 g) salt

To make your dough, on a wooden cutting board or on your clean countertop, make a mound with your flour and dig out a crater in the middle. Crack the eggs into the crater. Add the garlic, salt and black pepper to the eggs. Use a fork to carefully beat the eggs, making sure to fix the flour as it moves so you keep a mound shape. With your hands, start working flour into the eggs until the mixture starts to form a very sticky dough. Keep adding little bits of the flour into the mix, until you have a dough that is sticky but flexible enough to work with. It's really important you don't add too much flour, because the dough has to be light. Knead the dough with your hands for 3 to 5 minutes. This is one time where it's great to be "kneady"—this step is crucial to the ravioli coming out right. Wrap it in plastic wrap and sit it on the counter for 20 minutes to rest.

In a blender or food processor, blend the spinach, Parmesan cheese and ¼ cup (60 ml) of the olive oil. Add more olive oil, a little at a time, until the consistency is pasty, but not watery. This pesto is going to be your filling, so you don't want it to be runny.

Fill a medium-size pot with water and bring to a boil over high heat. Put a few pinches of flour on the cutting board or countertop and place the dough on it. Use a rolling pin or a glass to roll out the dough. Be careful and take your time. You need the dough to be thin enough so that you can almost see through it. Get a medium-sized drinking glass, and use the open end like a cookie cutter to cut circles out of the dough. Remember, you need an even number. Cut out the circles as close to one another as you can. When you can't cut out any more, reroll the scraps into a ball and repeat the rolling and cutting processes.

Put a small spoonful of the filling in the center of half of the dough circles. Top each filled circle with one of the remaining circles of dough and use a fork to carefully seal the edges all around. Drop the ravioli gently into the boiling water. Cover the pot and let them cook for 20 minutes, or until they float to the top and feel tender. Remove them with a slotted spoon and drain in a strainer or colander while you make the gravy.

Empty the water in the pot and return the pot to medium heat. Add the leftover meat stock. In a small bowl, mix the cornstarch with the water thoroughly. Add this to the stock and stir in the remaining salt. Cook, stirring to make sure the bottom doesn't burn. When the gravy is thick, remove from the heat. Plate the ravioli, pour the gravy over it and off you go!

HEALTHY MEALS
FOR HUNGRY MEN

GOOD FOR YOU FOOD THAT TASTES GREAT

Great food doesn't have to be bad for you, and these recipes prove just that! I always say that healthy cooking is what separates the boys from the men in the kitchen, as you leave the flavors naked with no mayo and sugar to cover it all up. There's a lettuce wrap recipe (see p. 143) that will replace any sandwich or taco you love with a healthier and fresher alternative. Tabbouleh salad made with quinoa (see p. 145) is a classic made gluten free. The key lesson is that you don't have to abandon your favorite recipes; you just have to find healthy alternatives to sub in for the heart-slowing, blood-pressure-raising ingredients we've all come to love.

GINGER SALMON

Fish is so good for you, and if you like it, so good to eat. I'm a big fan of salmon and don't like messing with it too much. Great-tasting salmon is more about cooking it perfectly than about soaking it in soy sauce. This sauce is light and sweet and easy to make.

MAKES 1 SERVING

1 tbsp (13 g) sugar
1 cup (240 ml) water
1 tsp (2 g) ground ginger
1 (8-oz [230-g]) salmon fillet, skin on
Pinch of salt

Preheat the oven to 375°F (191°C).

In a small saucepan over medium-high heat, whisk the sugar, water and ground ginger together. Cook, stirring every minute or so to keep the sugar from burning, for about 5 to 7 minutes, or until the sauce is sticky enough to coat the fish.

Use a pastry brush, a plastic spatula or your clean fingers to cover the top of the fish with the sauce. (Just the top; you won't be eating the skin, bud.) Season with the salt.

Put the salmon on a baking sheet and put it in the oven. Bake for about 20 to 25 minutes (depending on how thick it is), until it flakes apart with a fork and is light pink (salmon color, right?) all the way through. Dark pink is a sign it's not ready. Use a spatula to take your salmon off the baking sheet, leaving behind the skin. It's not fun to scrape the skin off the sheet, but the recipe makes for an awesome piece of salmon.

SMOKED CHICKEN SALAD LETTUCE WRAPS

Layers—it's all about the layers of flavor, whether it's a great lasagna, a sandwich or a wrap. I like to slow-cook chicken with liquid smoke and BBQ sauce to give it that great smoky flavor without the hassle of using a smoker. I make my own sauce or use Sweet Baby Ray's, but whatever you like is cool. Once your chicken is done and tastes awesome, why not apply it to the simplest leftover chicken dish ever—chicken salad? Finish it in a lettuce wrap to avoid the carbs and get the crunch.

MAKES 2 SERVINGS (5 LETTUCE WRAPS)

1 tsp (5 ml) liquid smoke
½ cup (120 ml) BBQ sauce
2 bone-in chicken quarters
1 cup (240 ml) water
½ white onion, diced fine
¼ cup (55 ml) mayo
¼ cup (31 g) canned corn, drained
1 tsp (2 g) paprika
5 leaves Boston or Bibb Lettuce
½ cup (56 g) shredded jalapeño
Jack cheese (optional)

Stir the liquid smoke into the BBQ sauce. Put the chicken in a slow cooker and cover the chicken quarters with the BBQ sauce mix. Add the water to the slow cooker and cook on high for 6 to 8 hours. The longer the better: just add more water if the liquid level gets too low. If you don't have a slow cooker, you can preheat your oven to 225°F (107°C) and cook the chicken in an ovenproof pot covered well with foil for 6 to 8 hours.

It doesn't really matter whether the chicken is hot or cold; I like it both ways. (I heard it, but I didn't mean it.) Use a fork to pull the meat off the bones and pull apart into small shreds. If the pieces don't pull apart as easily as you'd like, use a knife to cut them up. In a mixing bowl, mix the chicken with the onion, mayo, canned corn and paprika. Mix it up really well, so everything is evenly distributed.

Spread out the lettuce leaves on a plate. Boston lettuce is awesome for this because it's soft and flexible, but crispy and crunchy. Divide the chicken salad evenly between the lettuce leaves. Add the cheese—if you want to—and go to town!

BAKED GREEN TOMATOES AND PAN-SEARED PORK CHOP

Pork isn't the most healthful protein, but it's also not the worst and it will make for a tasty treat without completely breaking your healthy regimen. These green tomatoes are a nice change of pace from the usual vine-ripe and are much better for you than their deep-fried counterparts.

MAKES 1 SERVING

2 green tomatoes
½ cup (120 g) cornmeal
Pinch of granulated garlic
2 pinches salt
½ cup (120 ml) olive oil
1 (6-oz [170-g]) pork chop
1 tsp (2 g) black pepper

Preheat the oven to 375°F (191°C).

Cut the ends off the tomatoes and toss. Slice the tomatoes about ¼-inch (6 mm) thick. In a shallow bowl, mix together the cornmeal, garlic and a pinch of salt. Pour ¼ cup (60 ml) of the oil into another shallow bowl. Dip each tomato slice into the olive oil and then into the cornmeal mix and place on a baking sheet. Put the baking sheet in the oven and bake for 20 minutes.

Meanwhile, heat the remaining ¼ cup (60 ml) of olive oil in a frying pan over high heat. When the oil is very hot, in about 2 minutes, season the pork chop on both sides with a pinch of salt and the black pepper and place it into the pan. Cook for 2 minutes on each side and place it on the baking sheet with the tomatoes. Turn the tomatoes and cook them with the chop for about 25 minutes or until the chop is cooked through.

GLUTEN-FREE TABBOULEH

When I first opened the Chubby Chickpea, tabbouleh was the one Middle Eastern food on the menu that I hadn't grown up eating and knew very little about. Customers would make suggestions, but I still struggled to create the flavor that I thought would represent us well. One customer on a gluten-free diet suggested that we switch from the traditional bulgur (cracked wheat) to quinoa. And an Israeli cook I hired thought of tabbouleh as a mishmash of whatever greens and grains he liked best. Both of them inspired me to create this tabbouleh, which has all of my favorite salad things in it. The most time-consuming part of making tabbouleh salad is all the chopping. You obviously don't have a prep staff to do the heavy lifting, but I'd still recommend you chop everything by hand and not use a food processor. It will take longer but make a big difference in the taste. Don't beat yourself up about how fine you cut your veggies and herbs; the tabbouleh will be good anyway.

MAKES 2 SERVINGS

½ cup (92 g) quinoa

½ cup (120 ml) water

½ cup (20 g) finely chopped fresh flat-parsley

½ cup (20 g) finely chopped fresh cilantro

1 tbsp (7 g) finely chopped fresh mint leaves

1 tbsp (10 g) finely chopped tomato

1 tbsp (7 g) finely chopped cucumber

1 radish, sliced thin

Juice of 1 lemon

1 tsp (5 g) salt

1 tsp (2 g) cracked black pepper

1 tsp (3 g) granulated garlic

Cook the quinoa according to the instructions on the package. I cook quinoa with equal parts quinoa and water on low heat, covered, until the water is all gone. When it's done, spread it out on a baking sheet to cool.

Combine the parsley, cilantro and mint in a medium-size bowl. Mix them thoroughly with your clean hands. Add the tomato, cucumber and radish and mix it all again. Now add the lemon juice and seasonings, mixing again. Finally, add the quinoa and mix one last time. Good to go!

LURTING AVENUE ASPARAGUS

The best part of a two-religion family is experiencing the holidays you didn't grow up with and for me that's Xmas and Easter in the Bronx. My wife's family is as Italian as it gets, and they serve it up right—ham, lamb, filet, *prosciutto e melone*, pizza rustica—you name it. My favorite? The lightly breaded asparagus they bake off just before dinner is served. At my house, Christmas comes twice a week!

MAKES 2 SERVINGS

1 bunch asparagus
1 tsp (5 ml) olive oil
½ cup (60 g) dry Italian-style bread crumbs
¼ cup (45 g) grated Parmesan cheese

Preheat the oven to 375°F (191°C).

Break the ends off the asparagus spears: Bend each one, until the end snaps off about three-quarters of the way down from the tip. In a mixing bowl, toss the asparagus with the olive oil. Place the spears on a baking sheet and sprinkle bread crumbs and Parmesan over the asparagus. Bake for about 25–30 minutes, but keep an eye on them—they're done when they're slightly brown and look a little crispy.

HEALTHY JOES

Going back to the basics, a sloppy joe is a quick-and-easy way to make a tasty sandwich. I switched the burger meat out for ground turkey, used a wheat roll and stayed as far away from canned tomato sauce as is humanly possible. I do add Parmesan cheese, which isn't too bad as far as cheeses go!

MAKES 1 SERVING

1 tbsp (15 ml) olive oil

8 oz (230 g) ground turkey

1 cup (161 g) chopped tomatoes (if canned, buy no salt added)

½ white onion, chopped

½ jalapeño pepper, diced

Pinch of salt

1 tsp (2 g) black pepper

1 tsp (5 g) grated Parmesan cheese

1 bakery-fresh wheat roll

Heat the olive oil in a medium-size frying pan over medium heat. Add the turkey and cook, breaking it apart with a wooden spoon. Add the tomatoes, onion, jalapeño, salt, pepper and Parm, and stir really well. Reduce the heat to medium-low, cover the pan and cook, stirring occasionally, for about 20 minutes, or until the meat and sauce have gotten thick enough to scoop up with a spoon.

Toast the roll in a toaster oven (or in the oven at 350°F [177°C] if you have to) until it's the way you like it. Put the roll on a plate and pile the meat and sauce high on the roll.

BROWN SUGAR COUSCOUS WITH PAN-FRIED TILAPIA

Pairing a powerful side with a simple, clean protein works really well and leaves you with a balanced meal. Tilapia is a fish with a mild flavor and it's treated simply here, so the sweet and fruity couscous really shines. Couscous is an easy starch to make for dinner, and the tilapia cooks real fast.

MAKES 1 SERVING

½ cup (84 g) couscous
¼ cup (40 g) chopped dried apricots
1 tbsp (14 g) minced fresh ginger
1 tbsp (13 g) brown sugar
2 tbsp (14 g) chopped toasted cashews
2 tbsp plus 1½ tsp (40 ml) olive oil
2 pinches salt
1 (5-oz [140-g]) tilapia fillet, skinned
Pinch of black pepper

Make the couscous by following the directions on the package. When ready, transfer to a medium-size bowl and add the apricots, ginger and brown sugar. Fluff the couscous with a fork and mix in the chopped cashews. Add 1½ teaspoons (8 ml) of the olive oil and a pinch of salt and fluff again.

Heat the remaining oil in a medium-size frying pan over medium heat. Season the fish with a pinch of salt and a pinch of black pepper. Brown the fillet on both sides, turn the heat down to medium-low, and cook for 4 to 5 minutes, or until it flakes with fork and is cooked through.

NUTTY CHICKEN

This is a really basic, Asian-inspired dish that I like to make when I want something light but satisfying. Cauliflower can be really buttery and sort of resembles mashed potatoes when you're eating it as a side. No, it's not as heavy and creamy, but it's nice to have something on your fork other than chicken!

MAKES 1 SERVING

½ cup (120 ml) reduced-sodium soy sauce

1 tsp (2 g) ground ginger

2 pinches salt

1 (8-oz [230-g]) boneless chicken breast half

1 tsp (5 ml) margarine

2 cups (459 g) cauliflower florets

1 cup (240 ml) water

¼ cup (28 g) whole cashews

Preheat the oven to 400°F (204°C).

In a large zipper-top plastic bag or plastic container, mix the soy sauce, ground ginger and a pinch of salt. Cut the chicken open along one side, three-quarters of the way through, so that it opens like a clam or a book. Put the chicken into the bag or container and toss it around in the marinade. If possible, let it marinate for at least 30 minutes in the fridge.

Meanwhile, melt the margarine in a small saucepan over medium heat. Toss in the cauliflower whole along with a pinch of salt. Add the water, cover the pot and cook, stirring every 4 or 5 minutes to make sure the cauliflower doesn't burn, for about 25 minutes, or until soft enough to mash with a fork. Mash the cauliflower and mix in the cashews.

Take the chicken out of the marinade, setting the marinade aside. Put the chicken on a baking sheet or in a cast-iron skillet. Open the flap you cut earlier and, using clean hands, stuff the cauliflower and cashews into the chicken. Set any leftover stuffing aside. If you have butcher twine, tie the chicken closed. If not, just close it as best you can. Put the chicken into the oven for 30 to 35 minutes, or until cooked through. Make sure to check the bottom half, below the stuffing!

Put the marinade in a clean saucepan and cook on medium heat, uncovered, until it cooks down and thickens, stirring occasionally to make sure it doesn't burn on the bottom,. Make sure that the sauce boils a little bit—it had raw chicken in it and otherwise won't be safe to eat, bro.

Once everything is ready, microwave any extra cauliflower stuffing until warm and put it on a plate. Put the chicken on top of it, and pour your sauce over all. Delicious.

ALMOST MEAT LOAF

No question red meat is something worth avoiding if you're trying to be heart healthy. Meat loaf is tasty because it's fatty and juicy. So when you switch to turkey, you need to find a way to keep it juicy. My sister uses zucchini to keep a turkey loaf from drying out. She also uses BBQ sauce, but let's skip the sugar and rock with stone-ground mustard instead.

MAKES 2 SERVINGS

½ zucchini

1 lb (455 g) ground turkey

Pinch of salt

Pinch of black pepper

2 tbsp (31 ml) stone-ground mustard

Preheat the oven to 350°F (177°C).

Peel and then shred the zucchini into a large bowl using a cheese grater. If you don't have a cheese grater, cut the zucchini as small as you can or use a food processor and pulse until finely chopped. Don't let the zucchini turn into paste. Add the turkey, salt, pepper and mustard to the zucchini and mix it all together.

Coat a baking pan or cast-iron skillet (anything ovenproof) with nonstick spray and add the turkey mix. Put it in the oven for 40 to 45 minutes, or until the middle is firm and a knife inserted in the middle comes out dry. The shallower the pan, the less time it will take to cook.

Cut it right out of the pan and enjoy.

(TURKEY) MEATBALLS AND SPAGHETTI (SQUASH)

Healthy eating isn't easy unless you have the right mind-set. Starting with your favorite foods and replacing a few key ingredients helps. Anyone who loves spaghetti is going to feel like squash doesn't fit the bill, but in its own way, spaghetti squash is pretty good stuff. Drop the heart-stopping red meat for some lean turkey, and you've got a New World/Old World fave.

MAKES 1 SERVING

1 spaghetti squash
2 tbsp (30 g) unsalted butter
1 clove garlic, minced
1 tsp (3 g) dry unseasoned bread crumbs
4 oz (115 g) ground turkey
2 vine-ripe tomatoes, chopped
½ white onion, peeled and sliced
2 tbsp (23 g) grated Parmesan cheese

Preheat the oven to 400°F (204°C).

Cut the squash in half lengthwise and put it on a baking sheet. Roast for 35 to 40 minutes. When it is ready, take it out of the oven and set aside until it's cool enough to handle.

Melt 1 tablespoon (15 g) of the butter in a medium-size frying pan over medium heat. Add the garlic and cook, stirring, for 2 minutes. Transfer most of the butter and all of the garlic to a medium-size bowl and add the bread crumbs and turkey. Using clean hands, mix it all up and form into balls—the size isn't important. Brown the meatballs in the tiny bit of butter left in the pan over medium heat. Add the tomatoes and onion and cook, stirring occasionally, until the tomatoes' juices start to fill the pan. Reduce the heat to low, cover the pan and simmer the meatballs and sauce.

Use a fork to scrape out the long stringy pulp of the spaghetti squash, pulling out the seeds. Put the stringy insides on a plate and top with the Parmesan cheese. Pour the tomato sauce and meatballs over the top and voilà—just like grandma used to make, sort of.

ORANGE CHICKEN

This is just a healthier way to do orange chicken without breading, frying and pumping the dish full of sugar. If you feel like being extra healthy, sub out the marmalade for fresh orange slices, but give it a little longer to become a sauce.

MAKES 1 SERVING

1 tbsp (15 ml) olive oil
½ white onion, chopped
8 oz (230 g) chicken tenders
¼ cup (60 ml) chicken stock
¼ cup (80 ml) orange marmalade
¼ cup (12 g) chopped scallions

Heat the olive oil in a medium-size frying pan over medium heat. Add the chopped onion and cook, stirring, for 3 minutes to start them browning. Add the chicken tenders and cook about 4 minutes per side, stirring often.

Remove the onion and chicken from the pan and set aside. Add the chicken stock to the pan and give it a few minutes to bubble up. Stir it well and mix in the marmalade. Return the chicken and onions to the pan and cover. Let the mixture cook for 5 to 7 minutes, or until the sauce has thickened a bit around the chicken.

Put the chicken on a plate and sprinkle the scallions on top.

GLUTEN FREE COCONUT ENCRUSTED CHICKEN

I don't eat gluten free, but a lot of my customers do, and I've created a few recipes over time that don't have any gluten. This one is actually really tasty, and I like it as much as recipes with gluten in them. It doesn't hurt that I'm a big fan of coconut.

MAKES 1 SERVING

½ cup (48 g) almond flour
¼ cup (19 g) unsweetened shredded coconut
Pinch of salt
1 egg
1 (6–8-oz [170–230-g]) boneless chicken breast half

Preheat the oven to 375°F (191°C).

In a shallow bowl, mix together the almond flour, shredded coconut and salt. Crack the egg into another shallow bowl, and beat it well with a fork until smooth.

Cut the chicken breast in half horizontally, so you have 2 chicken fillets that are thin but otherwise the same size the chicken breast was in the first place.

Coat each fillet in the egg and then in the flour mixture. Put the chicken on a baking sheet and bake for 35 to 40 minutes, or until golden brown on top and cooked through. You're ready to eat!

MEXICAN SHREDDED CHICKEN

This is a tasty and healthy adaptation of a great Mexican classic that lets you grub with no guilt. The seasoning and cheesiness is still great, but without nachos or a tortilla, it's a carb-free option. If today's a cheat day and you're looking to get down, just pour this over nachos and do it up.

MAKES 2 PORTIONS

1 lb (455 g) boneless chicken thighs

1 cup (161 g) chopped tomatoes

1 (15-oz [430-g]) can black beans, rinsed and drained

2 tsp (4 g) chili powder

2 tsp (10 g) salt

1 tsp (2 g) ground cumin

1½ cups (350 ml) chicken stock

1 cup (140 g) shredded lettuce

½ avocado, chopped

¼ cup (10 g) chopped fresh cilantro

Mexican hot sauce, such as Cholula, to taste

½ cup (120 ml) sour cream

½ cup (56 g) shredded pepper Jack cheese

Put the chicken thighs, tomatoes, black beans, chili powder, salt, and cumin in the slow cooker and add half of the chicken stock. The thighs should be covered by the stock; if not, add some water to cover them. Cook on high for 6 hours.

Take the chicken pieces out of the cooker and shred it with a fork. Mix it back in with the veggies in the slow cooker. Put the shredded lettuce in a salad bowl and pour the chicken mix over the lettuce and top with avocado, cilantro, hot sauce, sour cream and cheese. Feeling some extra will power? Skip the cheese for an even lower fat meal.

MEDITERRANEAN PASTA SALAD

Pasta may seem like the wrong thing to make for one person, because if you're going to boil the water, might as well make the whole box. This dish is perfect for when you make more pasta than you can eat in one sitting. Rotini works best, but spaghetti, angel hair, penne, rigatoni, farfalle, campanelle, ziti, whatever you have around would work. For the rest, just go to your local grocery store and pick up a little of whatever you need from the salad bar. It's cheaper and more convenient than keeping a bunch of extra jars in the fridge.

MAKES 1 SERVING

2 cups (280 g) cooked rotini pasta, or 1½ cups (174 g) dried

2 tbsp (30 ml) olive oil, plus extra if cooking the pasta

½ cup (90 g) black olives

½ roasted red pepper from a jar, drained and chopped

½ cup (55 g) crumbled feta cheese

1½ cups (265 g) fresh spinach

1 tbsp (15 ml) balsamic vinegar

If you don't have any leftover pasta hanging around, put the dried rotini into a saucepan of boiling water (with a drop of olive oil in it) and cook according to the package directions. Drain the pasta and run cold water over it to help it cool down and keep it from getting stuck together.

Put the leftover or freshly cooked pasta into a medium-size bowl. Add the olives, pepper, and feta to the pasta and mix it up by lightly lifting the pasta with a fork 10 to 15 times.

Put the spinach on a dinner plate and pour the pasta on top. Drizzle lightly with the 2 tablespoons (30 ml) of olive oil and the vinegar and dig in!

BRUSSELS SPROUTS AND TURKEY BACON SALAD

Need fiber and protein without the carbs and extra calories? Try this quick warm salad. The turkey bacon gives the brussels sprouts a little bit of a salty kick and the pan-frying gives the whole dish a nice crispy quality!

MAKES 1 SERVING

6 strips turkey bacon

2 tbsp (30 ml) olive oil

1 small onion, chopped

10 brussels sprouts, halved

½ head cauliflower, trimmed, leaving just the florets

1 tbsp (9 g) garlic powder

2 tbsp (30 ml) water

1 (12-oz [340-g]) can chickpeas, rinsed and drained

Put a large frying pan on high heat. Cut the bacon into bite-size pieces and throw them in the pan. Add the olive oil and turn the heat down to medium. Add the chopped onion and cook, stirring until the onions are translucent and the bacon is crispy. Add the brussels sprouts, cut-side down, if possible. Add the cauliflower florets and season with the garlic powder. Stir it up, add the water and cover the pan. Cook for about 5 minutes.

After the veggies and bacon have cooked a bit, remove from the heat and add the chickpeas. Stir for 1 minute so the chickpeas get warm. Put the mix in a bowl and eat it up!

SPINACH CAPRESE PASTA SALAD

This is a quick-and-easy pasta salad recipe with fresh ingredients and clean protein. The tomatoes and mozzarella have a light and fresh taste, and the basil brings it all home. If tuna isn't something you're into, toss a can of chickpeas into the mix instead.

MAKES 1 SERVING

1 cup (140 g) cooked pasta shells

1 tbsp (15 ml) olive oil, plus extra if cooking the pasta

1 (5-oz [142-g]) can tuna, packed in water

¼ cup (23 g) sun-dried tomatoes

¼ cup (10 g) fresh basil

2 large handfuls of spinach

½ cup (56 g) shredded mozzarella cheese

1 tbsp (15 ml) balsamic vinegar

If you don't have any leftover pasta shells, put the dried shells into a saucepan of boiling water (with a drop of olive oil in it) and cook according to the package directions. Drain the pasta and run cold water over it to help it cool down and keep it from getting stuck together. Set aside.

Open the can of tuna and drain out the water. If the tomatoes are in a jar, take them out and drain them, too. Set aside.

Roughly chop the spinach and basil. Add the spinach and basil to a bowl with the pasta, tuna, tomatoes and cheese. Mix thoroughly and then drizzle the vinegar on top. Enjoy!

TAKING STOCK
IMPORTANT INGREDIENTS TO KEEP ON HAND

The biggest difference between my kitchen and those of my buddies has always been the basic things we've kept around just because we might need them. When you're trying to cook fresh and tasty food, it helps to have good ingredients lying around. And these recipes will be a lot less daunting if you have these key ingredients around.

SALT: It seems stupid to list this, but not everyone keeps salt in the house. Next time you're at the store, grab some kosher salt and some regular table salt and keep them in a cabinet. Everything you cook needs a little bit.

BLACK PEPPER: It doesn't matter if it's peppercorns you will grind yourself or ground black pepper; buy some and have it around. Black pepper and salt make the biggest difference in flavor; they go a long way.

GRANULATED GARLIC: I try to pick up fresh garlic whenever I'm at the grocery store and I would tell you to do the same. Thing is, it's expensive when you figure it doesn't last forever, and the granulated version is almost always a good substitute. Garlic is one of my go-to seasonings, and it can kick most dishes up a little bit.

FRESH VEGGIES: Carrots, celery, onions—these are the source of so many natural flavors and can be added to almost everything you cook. You don't have to get a lot, but make it a habit to pick up a small amount every two weeks or so. It's amazing the difference chopped onion will make in the simplest dishes.

OLIVE OIL: This is the most expensive key ingredient I use, and it sucks how much I use at my house. Thing is, it's better for you than butter, easier to use and tastes great in almost any panfried recipe. Look for sales and stock up; the stuff lasts forever and it's something you should never run out of.

CANOLA OIL: A lot of dishes you make, especially if you're frying something that is breaded, will use a vegetable oil instead of olive oil. It costs way less and having it on hand will save you money in the long run.

Some advice: I do my very best to run my kitchens as zero-waste work spaces, and I try really hard to do the same at home. This means buying only what I'm planning to use and finding uses for every part of the ingredients I buy. An example of this is deli meat or cheese; I go to the deli counter and order a specific number of slices. Most people make sandwiches all week, but order sliced turkey by the pound. How does that make sense? If you have 5 sandwiches and 2 slices of roast beef per sandwich, just tell the guy at the deli counter you need 10 slices, right?

Buy chicken or beef for a specific dish, and find other recipes that use the same protein, which you can make a few days in a row. Nothing is more expensive than a fridge full of leftover and unused raw protein—nothing! I've never been a planner, but I've seen the light! Hopefully you'll find that this book uses a lot of the same ingredients and steps in many recipes, so you'll be able to master a few techniques and be able to use ingredients in more ways than you have before.

ACKNOWLEDGMENTS

Life in food is not only a back-breaking labor of love for those of us who choose to live it, but even more so for the family and friends who support our dreams and endeavors. People who know and, sometimes, love me will tell you that it's especially hard being in my corner as I chase each and every exciting project that comes across my plate. I'd like to start by thanking my dad, Yona Shemtov, for not only instilling in me a deep understanding of flavors and textures but also, more importantly, for passing on the love of feeding people that was, and is, in his bones. My mom, Diane Shemtov, and my sister, Ronitte, for all of their help not only with this book but also with the Chickpea and too many festivals and catering events. My cousin Britney White, for all of her help and love. You're the very best! All of my friends who post and follow my passions on social media, pat me on the back and eat all of the crazy things I ask them to try. Mark and Rodi for believing in me and putting their money where their mouth is. My team at The Chubby Chickpea for keeping my dream alive, and my good friend David Harnik for many hours of unbilled consulting. Thank you all for everything you have done and continue to do to make all of this possible. Laura Days, thank you for all of your care and perspective on this book.

I'd also like to thank the folks at Page Street Publishing. From the very beginning of this process, you have all been so helpful and patient, teaching me so much as we've worked together. Your guidance on this project has brought my ideas to life, and I can't thank you enough for that.

Chef Andy Husbands for making this dream come true.

Ken Goodman, you are the man! Your photography took humble dishes and made them look extraordinary, and your passion for food helped shape this book—thanks a lot, buddy!

Matt Cohen, you have been an amazing friend, investor and partner. Without you, I'd be lost, bro.

Last, I'd like to thank my wife, Adrien, and our beautiful children, Adley and Adina. The investments that are made when a restaurant is built are immense, and no one has put as much into my projects as my family. Besides, if it wasn't for you, I'd be reading a book like this instead of writing it!

ABOUT THE AUTHOR

AVI SHEMTOV is the chef and founder of The Chubby Chickpea, a Boston-based food truck and suburban restaurant. He is also a proud father of two. Since graduating from the University of Massachusetts, Boston, with a degree in ethical, social and political philosophy, Avi has worked in sales and in the food service industries. In addition to food, Avi's passions include family, sports of all kinds and beating anyone he faces at board games.

INDEX

641.5611 SHEMTOV
Shemtov, Avi,
The single guy cookbook :
R2003004732 NRTHSD

NORTHSIDE

Atlanta-Fulton Public Library

SEP   2015